READING
ON
PURPOSE

READING
ON
PURPOSE

· ·

**Building
Cognitive Skills
for Intermediate
Learners**

**Fraida Dubin
Elite Olshtain**

▼▼**Addison-Wesley Publishing Company**

Reading, Massachusetts • Menlo Park, California
Don Mills, Ontario • Wokingham, England • Amsterdam • Bonn
Sydney • Singapore • Tokyo • Madrid • Bogota • Santiago • San Juan

A Publication of the World Language Division

Project Coordinator: Kathleen Sands-Boehmer
Manufacturing/Production: James W. Gibbons
Permissions: Merle Sciacca
Design: Ligature, Inc.
Cover Design: Marshall Henrichs

Printed in the United States.

ISBN 0-201-11671-5
FGHIJKLMNO-AL-99876543210

Contents

Part 1
Reading for Facts and Opinions

Unit One
Keeping One's Own World in a New World

Unit Two
Your Place in the World: Employment

Part 2

Reading for Ideas and Viewpoints $\quad$ 83

Introduction

To the Teacher

The Objectives

The concept for *Reading on Purpose* opens up new vistas in materials for ESL and EFL reading courses. At the start, our goal was to produce a book that fits a level between *Reading by all Means* (Dubin and Olshtain, 1981) for advanced learners, and *Three Easy Pieces* (Dubin and Olshtain, 1984) for low-intermediate. But every textbook writing project takes on its own special characteristics. Thus, in the preparation of this third book we were able to develop new ideas which make *Reading on Purpose* not just the filler between two other books, but one with a unique character of its own.

The focus in *Reading on Purpose* is reading for *meaning,* or reading in order to use information and ideas. This objective calls for an overall design which helps ESOL learners to develop:

1) thinking processes and cognitive skills necessary for meaningful reading;
2) general background knowledge necessary for comprehension of the text;
3) sensitivity to the features of different types of reading materials;
4) vocabulary understanding to derive meaning from the text;
5) experience in successful, sustained reading of interesting texts; and
6) a taste for reading enjoyment which can eventually lead to reading for the sake of reading.

To best fit the needs of the audience at the intermediate-advanced level, we decided that the selections should be unedited and "authentic" (unlike those in *Three Easy Pieces*); but also shorter, less specialized, and less exclusively for students in higher-education than those in *Reading by all Means*. At the same time, we have incorporated the focus on skills and strategies which has made *Reading by all Means* highly successful and widely copied, along with providing the motivation for reading fluently, the motif in *Three Easy Pieces*.

The Plan

Parts 1 and 2 move from a focus on topics of practical concern, emphasizing facts and information, to broader spheres dealing with both personal and ethical issues. Part 3 is specifically arranged in such a way that topics from Part 2 are recycled but in quite different contexts. In reading Part 3, learners thus utilize their previous knowledge and also extend their knowledge in new directions. Part 4 leads learners into making their own choices of reading materials.

The Units are each composed of three to five selections which are related by a common topic or thematic thread. Often, information in one selection is restated in one of the others in the same unit. Each unit begins with a section titled *Background Information* which orients learners to the common theme, frequently bringing in facts or ideas with which learners are already acquainted. The intention is to make learners aware of associating what they read in new materials with what they already know. Units Eleven, Twelve, Thirteen, and Fourteen specifically present topics from preceeding units. In each case, learners are led to recall, remember, and make use of their previous exposure to the topics.

The Selections are examples of natural, written language, or "authentic" materials. In order to give learners experience with reading a variety of text types, selections have been taken from newspapers, magazines, brochures and advertisements, textbooks and references, and non-fiction books. The final selection is from a novel which ranks as "literature." Since we do not believe the skill of reading is advanced by context-less materials, passages for the most part are taken from American English sources—although the works of at least two distinguished British writers, Bertrand Russell and Lawrence Durrell, are included. Topics have been selected for their universality in today's shrunken world; however, the cultural point of view is that of a contemporary reader within a world-wide, American English community. The topics chosen for *Reading on Purpose* were reviewed by many ESL teachers and their students. At best, though, reading topics selected for other people can never please everyone. For that reason, *Reading on Purpose* points learners towards discovering their own topics through the self-reading guides in Part 4.

The Exercise Materials are crucial to a reading skills text. *Reading on Purpose* tries to give enough to aid skill building, but not too much in order not to obscure the pleasure which can be derived from reading. Above all, attention has been paid to making the exercises challenging and motivating, never mechanical.

Pre-Reading Tactics: Acquaint learners with the characteristics of the text type; predict meaning before reading by attention to text features such as titles, sub-titles, the format, organizational elements in the writing, etc.

Vocabulary Awareness: Exposes learners to key expressions before reading by working on receptive knowledge of word meanings in the context in which they appear in the selection. Glossing is used for vocabulary items which cannot be guessed from context or are of more specialized nature.

Post-Reading Activities: Stress tasks which are cognitively-based such as the following: recalling and labeling information, analyzing ideas, applying information in new formats, categorizing and classifying information, evaluating ideas, synthesizing ideas, inferring and finding implied meanings, etc. They also give practice in strategies for reading such as skimming, scanning, guessing word meanings from the immediate context, using the organization of the writing for understanding, finding the writer's voice, etc. Many of the cognitively-based exercises lead to writing assignments, although *Reading on Purpose* does not attempt to give specific instruction in writing skills.

The approach in *Reading on Purpose* has been to design workouts which are dictated by the nature of the selection itself. Each selection was carefully examined with the question in mind: what will help learners understand the meaningful elements in this text? Thus, each Pre-Reading Tactics and Post-Reading Activities section is unique; some exercise types appear once or twice in the entire book, while others are repeated more frequently.

A Brief Teaching Guide

The units have been designed to follow each other sequentially, therefore they should be used in the order in which they appear in the text. Part 4, or attention to out-of-class, independent reading, should be introduced as early as possible.

Although ESL/EFL programs vary widely, students should be able to complete *Reading on Purpose* in a one semester course which meets 3-4 hours per week (average semester of 13-14 weeks). In courses that are limited to 1-2 hours per week, the materials in *Reading on Purpose* would suit a two semester program.

The teacher should introduce each unit, embellishing the "Background Information" section by bringing in references to events or issues of a local nature. Students then read this section silently. The teacher can lead a discussion which further motivates them to read the unit.

The teacher's input is also important in the Pre-Tactics section for each selection. The Pre-Tactics and the Vocabulary Awareness sections can be carried out by having the teacher lead a discussion with the whole class.

Next, students should read the selection independently with no further interruptions by the teacher.

The Post-Reading Activities should also be done individually. However, there are frequent instructions to work with a partner or in small groups. The teacher's role is important at this point as a director, making sure that each person has a suitable partner or is included in a group. Often it is effective for the teacher to join one of the groups.

After completion of the Post-Reading Activities, the teacher's role is to facilitate a wrap-up discussion or sharing of individual and small group results with the whole class.

Where Are The Answers?

We have decided not to include answers to exercise materials although, true enough, some teachers find them convenient. Our reasons are the following:

1) Answer keys give weight to the idea that there is always a "right" or "wrong" answer. We prefer that learners among themselves or with their teacher discuss, negotiate, and reach their own decisions on what is the best possible reply to a specific question.

2) Many, if not the majority of the activities in *Reading on Purpose* lead learners into *using* facts and ideas, thus making an answer key beside the point.

3) Presenting an answer key in a textbook abets testing of comprehension rather than building skills and knowledge. We strongly encourage the latter approach and wish to discourage "testing."

However, readers-users who want to discuss any of the exercises or who may be unclear about how to carry out any of the activities are encouraged to contact the authors c/o World Language Division, Addison-Wesley Publishing Company, Reading, Massachusetts 01867 USA.

The authors

READING
ON
PURPOSE

....

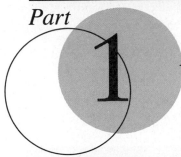

Part

1

Reading for Facts and Opinions

Unit One

Keeping One's Own World in a New World

Background Information for Unit One

Many major cities in the world today have large populations of people who have recently arrived; they have immigrated from other countries. Perhaps you, too, have left a familiar place to come to a new city or a new country. Or you may live in a city where there are large numbers of newcomers. Adapting to a new place forces people to seek out new friends, face new problems, and often learn a new language.

In this unit, you will read three selections that present different aspects of immigration, of what it means to move from one place to a new one. The first selection describes how students from many ethnic and cultural backgrounds get along with each other in a large, public high school in the Bronx, a part of New York City. At this school, young people who are 16–18 years old mingle with students from a number of backgrounds, even though they live in neighborhoods in New York which are populated, for the most part, by people who speak the same language and share the same cultural background.

But learning to live in a new land can be difficult, particularly for older

I Christopher Columbus High School **1**

people who find it hard to make cultural changes. Enrique Hank Lopez writes about how he felt when he was a boy in elementary school in Colorado, because his father, an immigrant from Mexico, had never learned how to read and write.

Newcomers to a country are looked on both negatively and positively, as the letter to the Editor of the *New York Times* suggests. Moreover, many countries in today's world have a growing percentage of foreign-born people, as the writer of the letter points out.

First Selection
Christopher Columbus High School A Mirror of New York

Pre-Reading Tactics

A. Before you begin reading this newspaper article, look at the form in which it was printed. Notice its many short paragraphs. Newspaper articles are often printed this way in order to help us read quickly. This article has a **title** and two **subtitles.** Read them carefully and try to understand their meaning.

1. The introduction to this unit stated that large cities such as New York have many ethnic and cultural groups, people who immigrated to the large city from other places in the world. What could "Mirror of New York" mean? How might Christopher Columbus High School mirror the city of New York?

    There are two subtitles in this reading selection:
    Bronx Changes Reflected
    Living With Prejudice

    Titles in newspapers do not usually follow regular grammatical rules; they give only the key words, letting the reader supply what is missing. Thus the title "Bronx Changes Reflected" actually means "the changes taking place in the Bronx area are reflected in Christopher Columbus High School." Notice that the word "reflected" can be used as "reflected in the mirror" or "reflected in one's ideas."

2. What do you think the second subtitle means: "Living With Prejudice"? Does it mean either:
   a. learning to accept the fact that there is prejudice or
   b. fighting against prejudice which exists around you.

B. Vocabulary Awareness—Learn the meaning of these **key expressions:**
   segregation
   racism/racial
   ethnic group
   prejudice
   Complete the **key expressions** in the following paragraph:

   "P＿＿＿ develops when people make judgments about other people without really knowing them or knowing about them. Therefore, p＿＿＿ is prejudgment. P＿＿＿ can be used against another e＿＿＿ g＿＿＿ or against a r＿＿＿ group. When p＿＿＿ is used against a r＿＿＿ group, r＿＿＿ might develop. R＿＿＿ of a stronger group against a weaker group often leads to s＿＿＿, which is really a severe separation between the groups. One way to avoid s＿＿＿ and p＿＿＿ is to encourage the different groups to mix and mingle.

C. Think about these questions while reading the selection:
   1. Does Christopher Columbus High School mirror segregation or a "mixing and mingling" of different ethnic groups?
   2. Who are the various groups that meet at school? How do they get along with each other?
   3. Where at school is the best meeting place for students of different backgrounds?

D. Read the article from beginning to end. You can understand the main ideas of this selection without using your dictionary for the unknown words. **Try it out!**

Christopher Columbus High School

A Mirror of New York

By Sara Rimer

1 Each day at lunchtime, when the students leave their assigned seats in the classroom, they re-create in the cafeteria the boundaries and divisions of the world outside Christopher Columbus High School.

2 Few people know the cultural and ethnic terrain of the cafeteria as well as John Watson, a *dean of boys,* who *presides* over the din of lunchtime. Walking among the rows of Formica-topped tables where the students sat eating lunch one day this term, he gave what seemed as much a tour of the Bronx as of the cafeteria.

3 "You've got your Arthur Avenue Italians over here," he said, pointing to a row at the far end. "Over there are your Morris Park Italians. Back there against that wall are your Hispanics. In the middle are your Parkchester blacks. Behind them are your Cambodians. Way in the back are your West Indian blacks."

4 Mr. Watson, his colleagues, and many of the students say the segregation that occurs in the cafeteria *stems* more *from* a universal desire to seek out the familiar than from racism.

5 "I don't think there's really any hatred," said Carmelina Pilla, who is the daughter of Italian immigrants. "It's just that people stay with their own groups— blacks with the blacks, Italians with the Italians, Spanish with the Spanish."

6 Just as the ethnic and cultural variety of the students accounts for some tension and the divisions in the cafeteria, so does it bring to the old brick school building in the Pelham Parkway section much of the *vitality* of the city itself. For six hours and eight minutes each day, people who rarely mingle in their own neighborhoods all come together—physically, if not always spiritually—under one roof.

7 "We have Spanish, we have Albanians, we have Koreans, we have people from New Jersey," said Violet Ademaj, a senior of Albanian descent as she enthusiastically describes her social studies class. "They all sort of blend in."

"It makes for a very fascinating atmosphere," Mr. Waston said.

Bronx Changes Reflected

8 "I wouldn't say there's love and harmony all over the place, because there are some *racial bigots,*" said Brenda Meltzer, the acting assistant principal for administration. "But there is *civility.*"

9 The black and Hispanic population at Columbus—once a school that was primarily Italian and Jewish—has gradually increased in the last 20 years, reflecting the changing population of the Bronx. Of the 2,800 students who were registered at the beginning of this school year, 1,300 were white, 721 Hispanic, 670 black and 101 Asian.

10 There are Albanian boys attending school and making a decent living as doormen on Park Avenue and Albanian girls who have al-

ready been promised in marriage to Albanian men chosen by their families.

11 There are the Arthur Avenue Italians, as they are called, from the sheltered Little Italy atmosphere of the Belmont section, with its family-owned bakeries and the melody of the Italian language floating along its narrow streets.

12 From another world are two of the school's celebrities—George and Darren Philip, virtuoso break dancers from East Tremont Avenue who miss school so they can go on European tours. Just back from Paris this term, George, who is 16 years old, took to Elizabeth Davidson's English class a color snapshot of himself breaking in front of the Eiffel Tower.

13 "Paris was great!" he told Miss Davidson. "But nobody spoke English."

14 There are always new immigrants going to Columbus and learning to speak English in Matthew DiLisio's beautiful classroom on the second floor, with the color pictures of America's monuments taped to the walls. Among the most recent arrivals are the shy Cambodians, boys and girls who survived the horrors of the Pol Pot regime.

●

15 "I suppose you'd like to go to a school with only white students," Grace M. Rosa, the principal, said, confronting a 16-year-old boy seated across from her during a *suspension hearing*.

16 "Yeah, I guess I'd have to go to Canada for that." He had been suspended for attacking a black student in the cafeteria with racial statements.

17 Mr. Watson later said the white student was one of a *handful* of graffiti writers who marked the walls with the initials WBIA—White Boys in Action. Other students generally look down upon the members of WBIA, dismissing them with such comments as, "They're a bunch of stupid kids."

18 The black student from the fight in the cafeteria was Charles Smith, a senior. He is among the *handful* of minority students who ride the subway to Columbus from the South Bronx—outside the official school zone—becaue his parents believe he will get a better education there than at the primarily black and Hispanic school to which he would normally be assigned.

Living With Prejudice

19 Charles said he had ignored the other boy's name-calling until he made a racial remark about some black girls sitting at a nearby table. "When he was speaking to me personally, it didn't bother me," he said. "But when he said that about those girls, all I could think of was, 'My girlfriend's black, my mother's black.'"

▶

dean of boys—similar to a headmaster

presides—supervises

stems from—comes from

vitality—liveliness

racial bigots—people who openly show their prejudice

civility—consideration (politeness)

suspension hearing—a meeting to decide if a student will be dismissed for a short time from school

handful—a small number

20   He said security officers broke up the fight after he had hit the other boy in the jaw. Both boys were sent to Mr. Watson's office. ''I had to talk to his mother on the telephone,'' Charles said. ''I told her, 'I'm sorry I hit him.' She said, 'I would've done the same thing.'''

●

21   Graca Misquitta arrived at Christopher Columbus last year as an obvious outsider—a girl from Bombay. ''I would say hi to a lot of kids, but they had their own groups,'' she said. ''Italians would speak to Italians, blacks would speak to their own kind. There weren't many Indians around. It was very lonely at first. My favorite pastime was going to the library.''

22   Everything changed last winter, when she made her first friend—Izabel Ginzbursky, whose family came from the Soviet Union four years ago. Graca and Izabel knew each other from biology class, where they scored the highest grades on most tests. Their friendship began, not in class, but in the cafeteria, which can be for newcomers one of the most *intimidating* places in the school.

23   ''I didn't have anyone to sit with because I was scared of making friends,'' Graca said. ''I was sitting all alone. Bella came up to me and said, 'Hi, I'm alone, too. Would you like to sit with me?'''

24   The friendship of Graca and Izabel soon grew to include other girls—Eun-Young Lee from South Korea; Gwendoline Patterson from the West Indies; Mini Guptan from a village in the south of India. Together they formed the group that has become known among the girls' parents and teachers as the League of Nations.

25   The girls say they are sad this spring because Mini is returning to India to enter medical school. But the others say they will stay together, at least for the next four years.

26   They all plan to enter the State University of New York at Stony Brook in the fall. Each girl has already chosen a career. Izabel wants to become a doctor, Graca a dentist, Eun-Young an engineer. Gwendoline wants to work with computers.

intimidating—frightening

Post-Reading Activities

A. Identify the Main Ideas:

True or False

1. _____ In the cafeteria students usually stay with people from the same background.
2. _____ In their classrooms students stay in their "assigned seats."
3. _____ WBIA is a small group which acts for better understanding among the different groups.
4. _____ Some of the boys at Christopher Columbus High School make a living by working after school.
5. _____ The fight between the white boy and Charles Smith had nothing to do with racism.
6. _____ The group of girls called the "League of Nations" prove that there can be close friendships among people from different backgrounds.

B. Discuss your answers for A (above) in a small group. Support your statements with examples from the article.

C. Find deeper levels of meaning by working with paragraphs:

1. Paragraph 1

The words "boundaries" and "divisions" used in the first paragraph emphasize:

a. separation.
b. variety.
c. nature.

2. Paragraphs 3 and 4

These paragraphs emphasize the fact that the cafeteria resembles the outside world because:

a. there is a lot of racism.
b. you cannot tell the differences among groups.
c. people like to stay with their own group.

3. Paragraph 6

By using the word "vitality," the author wants to emphasize the fact that different groups add:

a. a lot of tension.
b. interest and color.
c. hatred.

4. Paragraph 7

The expression "they sort of blend in" reflects the feeling that cultural and ethnic variety is:

a. a positive thing.
b. a negative thing.
c. something we should fight against.

5. Paragraph 8

By "civility" the assistant principal probably means that students from different backgrounds have learned to:

a. ignore each other.
b. accept each other.
c. love each other.

6. Paragraph 9

How has the population of the Bronx changed?

a. It has grown.
b. It has become more varied.
c. It has become smaller.

7. Paragraphs 10 and 11

These paragraphs emphasize the fact that outside the classroom, each ethnic group:

a. hates the other.
b. lives within its own cultural setting.
c. contributes to the variety of cultural backgrounds.

8. Paragraphs 15–18

These paragraphs tell about a case in which:

a. a white boy had to be suspended because he behaved like a racial bigot.
b. a black boy had to be suspended because he hit another boy.
c. parents take interest in what happens at school.

9. Paragraph 20

What did the white boy's mother mean when she said on the phone, "I would've done the same thing?"

a. That she agreed with her son.
b. That she agreed with the black boy.
c. That she would have suspended both boys from school.

10. Paragraphs 21–24

Graca and Bella became friends because they were both:

a. from the same ethnic group.

b. rather lonely.

c. angry at the other girls.

11. Paragraphs 25 and 26

One can tell how close a friendship the girls have developed from the way they:

a. meet in the cafeteria every day.

b. plan their future together.

c. are sad about the situation in the cafeteria.

D. Use new information:

1. Diagram 1 represents the student population of Christopher Columbus High School the way it is given in paragraph 9 in the article.

Diagram 1

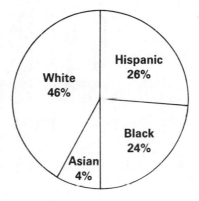

2. Fill in Table 1 with the names of the groups and the numbers of the students:

Table 1

Name of group	%	Number of students
	46%	
	26%	
	24%	
	4%	

3. Look at Diagram 2, which shows the increase in the percentage of racial and ethnic groups in the United States. After you have gone over the diagram carefully, fill in Table 2, which is similar to Table 1, to show which group increased most. Begin at the top with the group which increased least and continue down the line to the one which increased most.

D. **Discuss** in a small group or with a partner the affect the information given in your table above might have on the changes in American society.

Diagram 2 THE RACIAL AND ETHNIC ORIGINS

Asian-Americans are growing faster than any other single group—largely because of immigration.

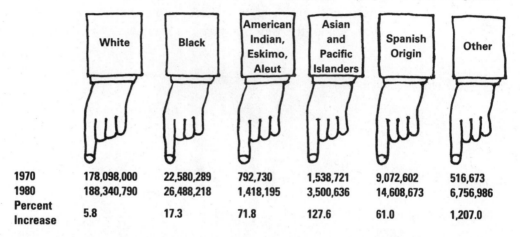

	White	Black	American Indian, Eskimo, Aleut	Asian and Pacific Islanders	Spanish Origin	Other
1970	178,098,000	22,580,289	792,730	1,538,721	9,072,602	516,673
1980	188,340,790	26,488,218	1,418,195	3,500,636	14,608,673	6,756,986
Percent Increase	5.8	17.3	71.8	127.6	61.0	1,207.0

*Using 1970 classification procedures, which were changed for the 1960 census, would have produced these approximate totals: whites, 195.1 million; blacks, 26.6 million, and Asians and Pacific Islanders, 3.3 million.   Source: Bureau of the Census

Table 2

Group	% of increase
	1.207%

The Problem of Fathers and Sons

Pre-Reading Tactics

A. This selection is also a newspaper piece but of a different nature. Notice that it too has many paragraphs, but they are longer than those in the previous selection. In this article the writer tells a story about his childhood; therefore, the beginning of each paragraph helps the reader keep the story line in mind by setting the *time,* the *background*, and the *relation* of what is going to be said in the new paragraph to what went on in the *earlier* paragraph.

B. **Skim** the article by reading only the first line in each of the first nine paragraphs. As you do so, try to answer the questions for each paragraph by filling in the missing words. (Remember! Read only the first line in each paragraph.)

1. **Paragraph 1**
   First sentence which is also the first paragraph. It introduces

   _____.

2. **Paragraph 2**
   begins with _____.
   These words give the time at which the story starts.

3. **Paragraph 3**
   begins with _____. It means approximately "as a result of what was said in the previous paragraph."

4. **Paragraph 4**
   begins with _____. This word often introduces some explanation relating to what was said earlier.

5. **Paragraph 5**
   is a single sentence which stands out clearly. Guess who "he" is in this sentence. (The answer is found in the first sentence of the story.)

6. **Paragraph 6**

begins with the pronoun "his" which refers to the same person mentioned in Paragraph 5. Who does it refer to? _____

7. **Paragraph 7**

begins with the word _____. This word which often appears in stories to indicate the time of an event.

8. **Paragraph 8**

It begins with a description in the progressive form, often used in stories to describe the background setting. When you read the first words, "Standing there in the dark," you get the feeling and atmosphere but you don't yet know *who* is there. What is the general mood in this

paragraph? _____

9. **Paragraph 9**

begins with the word _____. This word marks the passing of time.

C. Vocabulary Awareness—Learn the meaning of these **key expressions:**

illiterate—a person who does not know how to read and write
proficient reader—someone who reads very well
weekly pay check—weekly salary

The Problem of Fathers and Sons

by Enrique Hank Lopez

1 My father was an *articulate,* fascinating storyteller, but totally illiterate.

2 By the time I entered fourth grade, in Denver, Colo., I was a proud, proficient reader—and painfully aware of my father's inability to read a single word in either Spanish or English. Although I'd been told there were no schools in his native village of Bachimba, Chihuahua, I found it hard to accept the fact that he didn't even know the alphabet.

3 Consequently, every night as I watched my mother read to him I would feel a *surge of resentment* and shame. Together they bent over La Prensa from San Antonio, Texas—the only available Spanish-language newspaper. "How can he be so dumb?" I would ask myself. "Even a little kid can read a damned newspaper."

4 Of course, there were many adults in our barrio who couldn't read or write, but that was no comfort to me. Nor did it console me that my hero Pancho Villa was also illiterate. After all, this was my own father, the man I considered to be smarter than anyone else, who could answer questions not even my mother could answer, who would take me around the ice factory where he worked and show me how all the machinery operated, who could make huge cakes of ice without any air bubbles, who could fix any machine or electrical appliance, who could tell me all those wonderful stories about Pancho Villa.

5 But he couldn't read. Not one damned word!

6 His ignorance was almost too much for me to bear. In fact, whenever I saw my mother reading to him—his head thrust forward like a dog waiting for a bone—I would walk out of the kitchen and sit on the back porch, *my stomach churning* with a swelling anger that could easily have turned to hatred. So bitter was my disappointment, so deep my embarrassment, that I never invited my friends into the house during that after-dinner hour when my mother habitually read to him. And if one of my friends had supped with us—which happened quite frequently—I would hastily herd them out of the kitchen when my mother reached for La Prensa.

7 Once, during a period of deepening frustration, I told my mother that we ought to teach him how to read and write. And when she said it was probably too late to teach him—that it might hurt his pride—I *stomped* out of the house and ran furiously down the back alley, finally staggering behind a trash can to vomit everything I'd eaten for supper.

8 Standing there in the dark, my hand still clutching the rim of the can, I simply couldn't believe that anyone as smart as my dad couldn't learn to ▶

articulate—speaks well
surge of resentment—feeling of anger
my stomach churning—turning over
stomped—walked angrily

read, couldn't learn to write "cat" or "dog" or even "it." Even I, who could barely understand the big words he used when he talked about Pancho Villa *(revolucion, cacique, libertad, sabotaje, terreno),* even I, at the mere age of 10, could write big words in both English and Spanish. So why couldn't he?

9   Eventually, he did learn to write two words—his name and surname. Believing that he would feel less humble if he could sign his full name rather than a mere "X" on his weekly paycheck, my mother wrote "Jose Lopez" on his Social Security card and taught him to copy it letter by letter. It was a slow, painstaking process and usually required two or three minutes as he drew each separate letter with solemn tight-lipped determination, pausing now and then as if to make sure they were in the proper sequence. Then he would carefully connect the letters with short hyphen-like lines, sometimes failing to close the gaps or overlapping the letters.

10   I was with him one Friday evening when he tried to cash his paycheck at a local furniture store owned by Frank Fenner, a red-faced German with a bulbous nose and squinty eyes. My father usually cashed his check at Alfredo Pacheco's corner grocery store, but that night Pacheco had closed the store to attend a cousin's funeral, so we had crossed the street to Fenner's place.
"You *cambiar* this?" asked my father, showing him the check.
"He wants you to cash it," I added, annoyed by my father's use of the word *cambiar.*
"Sure, Joe," said Fenner, "Just sign your monicker on the back of it."
"Firme su nombre atras," I told my father, indicating that Fenner wanted him to sign it.

"Okay, I put my name," said my father, placing his Social Security card on the counter so he could copy the "Jose Lopez" my mother had written for him.

11   With Fenner looking on, a smirk building on his face, my father began the ever-so-slow copying of each letter as I literally squirmed with shame and hot resentment. Halfway through "Lopez," my father paused, nervously licked his lips, and glanced sheepishly at Fenner's leering face. "No write too good," he said. "My wife teach me."

12   Then, concentrating harder than before, he wrote the final *e* and *z* and slowly connected the nine letters with his jabby little scribbles. But Fenner was not satisfied. Glancing from the Social Security card to the check, he said, "I'm sorry, Joe, that ain't the same signature. I can't cash it."
"You bastard!" I yelled. "You know who he is! And you just saw him signing it."

13   Then suddenly grabbing a can of furniture polish, I threw it at Fenner's head, but missed by at least 6 inches. As my father tried to restrain me, I twisted away and screamed at him, "Why don't you learn to write, goddamn it! Learn to write!"

14   He was trying to say something, his face *blurred by my angry tears,* but I couldn't hear him, for I was now backing and stumbling out of the store, my temples throbbing with the most awful humiliation I had ever felt. My throat dry and sour, I kept running and running down Larimer St. and then north on 30th St. toward Curtis Park, where I finally flung myself on the recently watered lawn and wept into a state of complete exhaustion.

15   Hours later, now *guilt-ridden* by what I had yelled at my dad, I came

blurred by my angry tears—unclear because of my tears
guilt-ridden—feeling guilty

home and found him and my mother sitting at the kitchen table, a writing tablet between them, with the alphabet neatly penciled at the top of the page.

"Your mother's teaching me how to write," he said in Spanish, his voice so wistful that I could hardly bear to listen to him. "Then maybe you won't be so ashamed of me."

16   But for reasons too complex for me to understand at that time, he never learned to read or write. Somehow, the multisyllabic words he had always known and accurately used seemed confusing and totally beyond his grasp when they appeared in print or in my mother's handwriting. So after a while, he quit trying.

Enrique Hank Lopez, taught at Harvard's Institute of Politics, was an international lawyer and author of several books, including, "The Harvard Mystique."

Post-Reading Activities

A. Guess the words from the context:

1. Paragraph 2

"painfully" means:

a. very

b. somewhat

c. a little

2. Paragraph 9

"painstaking" means:

a. easy

b. enjoyable

c. difficult

3. Paragraph 11

"smirk" means an expression of:

a. interest

b. scorn

c. pleasure

4. Paragraph 12

"not satisfied" means that he was not ready to:

a. accept it

b. give him anything

c. make an effort

B. Discuss in pairs or groups:

1. How important are the skills of reading and writing?
2. Have you known anyone who was illiterate? What difficulties did the person have?

Third Selection

Immigrants Place No Strain on the American Environment

Pre-Reading Tactics

A. This selection is a letter written to the editor of a newspaper. From the **title,** you can see it deals with immigration in the United States. The writer of the letter is reacting to an article that had appeared previously. Two conflicting views are presented: one reflecting the writer of the article, the other that of the writer of the letter. While reading, compare these two points of view.

B. Vocabulary Awareness—The headline contains a key word which also appears in the first paragraph. That word is part of a phrase that the letter writer quotes from the article that appeared previously. Find the phrase and write it here:

" _____ "

Does the letter writer believe that immigrants place too large a burden (strain) on the environment of the U.S.?

Yes _____ No _____

Did the writer of the article think so?

Yes _____ No _____

Immigrants Place No Strain on the American Environment

To the Editor:

In an article on your May 8 Op-Ed page, Russell W. Peterson, president of the National Audubon Society, *rehashes* familiar myths about the dangers of "increasing population" in this country. Mr. Peterson advocates greater *restrictions* on immigration to this country and claims that our steadily increasing population is "straining the land's natural carrying capacity."

Such arguments *fly in the face of* the most elementary demographic facts. The truth is that the U.S. has a very low population density when compared with most similarly advanced industrialized countries (e.g., the Netherlands' and Japan's population density is 344 and 314 people per square kilometer, respectively, as against 25 for the U.S.).

Furthermore, in spite of the alleged burdensome number of immigrants admitted yearly into this country, the percentage of the foreign-born in our general population has decreased dramatically since the early part of the century, from 14.6 percent in 1910 to 4.7 percent in 1970. Countries like Great Britain, Sweden, Switzerland, France, Australia and Canada have a larger share of foreign-born people in their populations than the U.S.

As to the matter of environmental pollution, this can hardly be blamed on the relatively modest increase of our population. It is rather the result of carelessness and inadequate environmental protection measures.

There have been many spectacular improvements in environmental conditions in many countries in recent years, and they had nothing to do with population control.

Finally, the above issues do not even begin to address the profound moral and historical grounds upon which this country's generous immigration policies have stood ever since the Founding Fathers first declared this land a bastion of freedom.

To restrict immigration unduly would not only go against the very character of this country, it would deprive us of the great benefits we have derived from those uncounted immigrants who have made outstanding contributions to our social, cultural and economic life.

George P. Mann

The writer is an immigration lawyer.

rehashes—goes over familiar material
restrictions—limitations
fly in the face of—creates confusion

Post-Reading Activity

A. Discuss in pairs or groups. What is the letter writer's attitude toward these three main issues as related to immigration?
1. Population density
2. Environmental pollution
3. The special character of the American nation

B. Write a letter to the Editor. Do you agree with the letter writer (George P. Mann)? Or, do you agree with the author of the article (Russell W. Peterson, president of the National Audubon Society)?

Decide which side you are on. Then, write your own letter to the Editor. Explain why you support one view or the other. Share you letter with others in the class.

Unit Two

Your Place in the World: Employment

Background Information for Unit Two

To make decisions about a job or career, you often must choose between personal goals and responsibilities to others. A choice based on one's own need for fulfillment might be attractive but difficult to reach. On the other hand, a career decision which is based on following the traditions and needs of one's family might be less appealing but easier to achieve.

Each of the four selections in this unit contains a point of view on individual versus family or group responsibilities. In some cases the writer's position is clear; in others it is not stated but can be inferred. While you are reading, you should think about how the question of individual versus family goals affects your own life.

In the first selection, you will read practical information about getting a job through an interview, then in the second about women and careers. The first selection gives a number of suggestions for having a successful job interview, while the second one confronts the reader with the issue of women's roles, as a career-seeker or homemaker.

As you read all four selections in this unit, think, too, about the underlying goals they reflect: do they implicitly place value on achievement and success in the work world based on an individual's drive and ambition, or do they present other goals and values?

First Selection

Careful Preparation . . .

Pre-Reading Tactics

A. Skim the headline to find the main topic:

   1. To understand the headline, the reader must add one important word.
      What is it?
      Clue: Headlines often leave out forms of the verb *be*.

2. Rewrite the headline as a normal sentence by rearranging the order of the words and adding all the words that have been omitted. _____

_____.

B. Vocabulary Awareness—Learn the meaning of these **key expressions:**
The article appeared in a newspaper, not as a news item but as a news feature in which the writer uses many idiomatic and colloquial expressions that would be heard in an informal interview between the writer and an employment specialist.

Three important expressions are: *personnel, employment,* and *job.* All other **key expressions** in this passage relate to "personnel" and "job interviews." The word "personnel" refers to the body of persons employed in an organization. People whose profession it is to deal with

personnel matters are p_____ experts. Such experts who deal specifically

with employment are e_____ specialists or employment counselors who advise "job hunters" how to find (or land) a job with a "prospective"

employer. At a j_____ interview the interviewer asks the "job seeker" a lot of questions. Some of these questions are considered "loaded"

q_____ because the interviewer uses them to get more information than seems obvious from the questions. The objective of the interviewer is to

learn all about the weaknesses and the strengths of the j_____
s_____ s.

Careful Preparation, Keeping Cool, Keys to a Fruitful Job Interview, Experts Say

by William H. Wylie

1 WASHINGTON—This is the time when college graduates are busy with job interviews in the hope that four years—or more—of high-priced education was not in vain.

2 A job hunter can have the best credentials in the world and still *flunk* the job interview. If that happens, his dreams of employment are shattered, at least with one employer.

3 Some people are naturally better at interviews than others, thanks to an outgoing personality. But it takes more than a *glib line of gab* to land a job.

4 Preparation is the thing, say personnel experts. Learn how to *play the game* of hard questions, which is what a job interview is all about. Interviewers may differ in technique, but there are 10 or 12 questions most of them always ask.

5 The interview is considered so important in landing a job that Carnegie-Mellon University in Pittsburgh stages simulated sessions for MBA students and puts them on videotape, said Ed Mosier, director of placement for the Graduate School of Industrial Administration.

No Harmless Questions

6 "The first 60 to 80 seconds are the most important part of an interview," Mosier said.

7 "This occurs during the *small talk* before the hard questioning begins. If you can relate some unique experience that will make the interviewer remember you, it may clinch a job," he said.

8 "But it must be done without appearing to be contrived. I remember a girl who mentioned that she did macrame. So did the interviewer's wife."

9 Some of the questions seem harmless enough. Actually, they are tricks designed to bring out your weaknesses and strengths.

10 "Tell me about yourself" is almost always asked, employment counselor Carol Hershey says. "It's a trap for ramblers. The interviewer wants to see how quickly you organize your thoughts and how well you communicate. Someone who rambles all over the lot is on shaky ground."

11 Your answer also provides a glimpse of your character and interests. Hershey recalled an episode about a lawyer being interviewed for trial work with a large firm. "She talked about a skiing medal she had won. It showed she liked to win, an important quality for a trial lawyer."

12 Another question that usually catches people *off guard:* What are your weaknesses?

▶

flunk—fail
glib line of gab—smooth talk
play the game—know or do what is expected
small talk—light conversation
off guard—not prepared

13 "It's a most difficult question," Hershey said. "One should always try to present a weakness in a positive light. You might say, 'One of my problems is that I'm a perfectionist. It interferes with my personal life because I'm always taking work home.'"

14 Perhaps the most dangerous booby trap is the inquiry: What do you think of your former boss or company?

'Never Bad-Mouth'

15 Personnel specialists agree that it's a loaded question. "Never bad-mouth anyone," advises Hershey. "If you were fired, discuss personality conflicts, if that was a problem, without blaming anyone. Always stress that the conflicts didn't prevent you from doing your job well."

16 It's best to present a former boss in a positive light. It might be noted that "he helped me learn specific skills" or "he was under a lot of pressure." You might add, "But I would have handled it differently and shown more compassion to the employees."

17 Why didn't you do better in college?

18 This is another question designed to put the interviewee *on the defensive*. If your *mind goes blank*, you might stall for time, saying, "Could you be more specific?"

19 What do you expect for a salary?

20 Careful! This takes some *finesse*. If the question comes up at your first interview, be general. Dance around specific numbers. You might bounce the ball into the interviewer's court by saying, "What is the salary range?" Or you could suggest that if the company is really interested in hiring you, there shouldn't be any problem in getting together on compensation.

21 Personnel people say there are always four or five questions that people should be ready for. One is the old chestnut: Where do you expect to be in five years?

22 Mosier said the answer is important because it tells whether a person sees himself as a manager or a specialist.

23 Hershey advises a general reply. "It's better to say I want to be in a job where I can grow professionally and take on responsibilities."

24 Why do you want to work for us?

25 This is another subject that can be handled easily by doing some homework about the prospective employer. Displaying your knowledge about the corporation may make you stand out from other applicants.

26 There are always some soft questions—soft if you're prepared—like:

—Are you creative? Give three examples.

—Are you a natural leader? Give examples.

—Are you a good planner? Give examples.

—What were your outstanding achievements on your previous job?

—What makes you different from the other applicants?

bad-mouth—say something negative
on the defensive—in a position of having to justify
mind goes blank—cannot think of what to say
finesse—knowing the right thing to say

Post-Reading Activities

A. Guess the meaning of unknown words and expressions from the context:
Sometimes you can guess the meaning of words and expressions you do
not know by finding clues in the same sentence or paragraph. Here are
words from the selection one can guess by using the clues indicated.

1. Paragraph 2

new word: *shattered*

clue: the job hunter can flunk (fail) the interview . . . his

dreams of employment are _____

    a. fulfilled

    b. destroyed

    c. opened

2. Paragraph 10

new words: *ramblers, to ramble all over*

clue: someone who rambles . . . is on shaky ground

    a. going around a question

    b. stepping in the middle

    c. avoiding a question

3. Paragraph 11

new word: *a glimpse*

clue: Hershey recalled an episode

    a. an indication of

    b. a failing in

    c. an opinion of

4. Paragraph 13

new word: *perfectionist*

clue: "I'm always taking work home."

    a. a perfect person

    b. a homebody

    c. a person who tries to do everything perfectly

5. Paragraph 16

new word: show more *compassion*

clue: I would have handled it differently

    a. give more understanding

    b. grade more seriously

    c. argue more intelligently

6. Paragraph 20

new words: *dance around*

clue: it's *not* a party, so dance around means:

      a. to not give exact information
      b. to wait to be invited to dance
      c. to decline an invitation

7. Paragraph 20

new words: *bounce the ball*

clue: it's *not* a tennis game, so bounce the ball means:

      a. to try out
      b. to give the other person the obligation to speak next
      c. to seek revenge

8. Paragraph 25

new words: *do some homework*

clue: it's *not* an interview in a school, so to do some homework means:

      a. making a telephone call
      b. reading a newspaper
      c. finding out everything you can about the company

B. Scan the selection to recall the major ideas:

Scan means to look back at a text you have already read or are familiar with to find specific information.

1. Tell me _____?
2. What are your _____? (Paragraph 10)
3. What do you think of _____? (Paragraph 12)
4. Why didn't you _____? (Paragraph 14)
5. What do you expect for _____? (Paragraph 17)
6. Where do you _____? (Paragraph 19)
7. Why do you want to _____? (Paragraph 21)
8. What were your _____? (Paragraph 24)
9. What makes you different from _____? (Paragraph 26)
10. Are you _____? Give some examples _____. (Paragraph 26)

C. Discuss with a partner:

Take turns being a job interviewer and an applicant. One asks the questions, the other gives replies. Try to follow some of the suggestions in the article for a fruitful job interview.

Second Selection

A Career Homemaker Looks at the Future

Pre-Reading Tactics

A. Read the **title** to understand the main theme of the article:

A person whose career is homemaking is a _____

_____.

B. Skim the article to find the overall idea:

To skim means to read rapidly for the main ideas, without stopping to look up new words and expressions in the dictionary. After skimming, answer this question:

Is the writer:

1. an older, married woman with a message for other older, married women?
2. an older, married woman with a message for men?
3. an older, married woman with a message for younger, married women?

C. Read the article from beginning to end. You can understand the main ideas without using your dictionary. Try it out!

A Career Homemaker Looks at the Future

by Diane Markam

1   What happens inside your head and your heart when the man whom you've learned to depend on finds his job so unbearable that he's driven to leave it, suddenly and without preparation?

2   We are, by today's standards, an old-fashioned family: four children, a mortgaged house, one of two cars paid for. Like many women with children, I chose to raise my offspring in person. I do photography, and make some money to complement the salary of my husband, Jack, but my checks are sometime things. I like this arrangement. Not long ago, however, I was forced to take a new and unsettling look at the way I've lived my married life.

3   I had no real preparation for the shock. Of course, I knew that Jack was under too much pressure at work. I knew that he couldn't enjoy what little time he had at home. I also knew that he was tense, unhappy and probably *courting a coronary*. But I didn't know that he'd take such a drastic step with so little warning. I could hardly believe it when he came home that day and told me, ever so gently, that he'd simply had enough. He had quit.

4   At first, I felt a fluttering sense of having stepped into fantasyland. Then I thought that this, after all, was Jack's job. It was his decision to make. He had made it hastily, although he wasn't ordinarily a rash person. Having felt desperate enough to quit, he should be free to do it. Besides, I thought, he might change his mind.

5   But Jack didn't change his mind—even though he'd been with his company for more than 10 years. He had risen through union ranks into management. With time, we'd gained a small measure of security. Now, without the company, all security vanished.

6   The profit-sharing plan, the regular bonus checks, the medical, dental and life insurance, the long paid vacations, the knowledge that when one paycheck went another would replace it—all these things were now gone, things on which we'd both depended. They were our livelihood, everything we'd planned on. Now, without any voice in the matter, I was cut off from my future, too. What had been our income was gone. It had never been ours, really, it had been Jack's. If I said that before, Jack always corrected me. ''Ours,'' he said. But time proved him wrong.

7   Disbelief and shock gave way to a sense of loss. Then anger boiled up in me. For my time had been invested as irretrievably as his. My life had been defined by the limits of our freedom and income. As family purchasing agent, I'd spent countless hours computing prices per ounce in crowded grocery stores and examining labels in boys'-wear departments. I'd shepherded, governed, stifled and substituted even my thoughts to fit the life-style that we could afford. Jack may have worked to make his salary, but I worked to make that salary work for us.

8   But my fringe benefits, my insurance, vacations and retirement benefits were all secondhand. I was subject to their limitations, yet I had no claim or control over them. Why had this never bothered me before? Per-

haps because I'd never been forced to think about it before.

9 No job comes with guarantees. Jack could have lost his job, and we'd have suffered an equal loss of investment. If I'd chosen to work outside the home, my job too would have been subject to the turns of circumstance. But, with my own job, I would never have found myself in that maddening limbo as the accidental victim of a falling out between Jack and "our" company.

10 I should point out that selfishness is hardly a motivating factor here. For, though I haven't brought the children into this examination of my own feelings, they do reside at the center of my concern. They're the reason I chose to remain at home. They, in fact, would be the losers if some catastrophe should strike while Jack's between jobs. And they're the reason that I worry about security.

11 I can't, however, find a target for my anger—an anger that shouldn't be focused on Jack. He, after all, is a human being, with a breaking point, like any other—a human being entitled to a freedom of choice. If I were in his position, I'd also feel that I must have the right to make a similar decision.

12 Perhaps I should be angry with myself. But clearly I'm not. No outside job could have given me the joys that my children have offered me.

13 In time my anger will no doubt *dissipate*. And our life will take on another style, and fall again into a routine. It may even turn out that everything has changed for the better.

14 But I don't think that I'll ever forget what I've learned in the days since Jack quit: that, in many ways, I and millions of other homemakers live in a fantasy world. Our working conditions and hours on the job are nonnegotiable. We *always* take our work home with us. And if we look closely at our economic compensations, we see only reflections.

15 After 15 years as a career homemaker, I've come to this realization late. Yet I better understand my younger sisters who question the wisdom of entrusting their economic future to someone else. It's a generous, romantic, idealistic and fundamentally unsound thing to do.

Diane Markam (a pseudonym) lives in California.

courting a coronary—doing things that might bring about a heart attack
dissipate—go away
pseudonym—not the author's real name

Post-Reading Activities

A. **Read** for main and supporting ideas. As you read for information, look for the sentences and sections that state the main points. At the same time, be aware of those sections that provide supporting or backup material.

This activity will guide you to the main ideas. With a partner, talk over your answers.

1. Paragraph 3

Who is the writer? _____

What was the crisis in her life?

_____

2. Paragraph 4

Does she feel he had a right to make the decision?

_____

3. Paragraphs 5, 6, 7

How does she feel? _____

Why does she feel this way? _____

4. Paragraphs 7, 8, 9

What had been her job in the family as homemaker?

_____

Was she consulted about the decision her husband made? _____

5. Paragraph 10

Why had she decided to be a full-time homemaker?

_____

Why does she reconsider that decision?

6. Paragraphs 11, 12, 13

Who is she angry with now? _____
What will happen with her anger in time?

_____?

7. Paragraphs 14, 15

What do homemakers always do? _____
What advice does she give to younger women?

_____

B. **Write** a summary, using the answers to A above. A sample summary appears below:

> The writer, a career homemaker, faces a crisis in her life when her husband quits his job, which is the family's primary source of income. The husband, his wife believes, had good reason to resign. Further, she feels it was his decision to make. However, she finds herself filled with anger because she no longer can enjoy the measure of security she had come to take for granted. She had managed the family's economic life but had not been part of the decision to cut it off. She reviews her reasons for

deciding to be a full-time homemaker despite the limitations of the job. Primary was her desire to be with the children while they were growing up. But the experience of losing the family's livelihood—even temporarily—makes her reconsider that decision. Now, she is not angry with her husband or with herself. Instead she speaks out to women fifteen years younger than herself by advising them not to place the economic basis of their lives in the hands of another person.

Third Selection
The Moth and The Star

Pre-Reading Tactics

A. The author of this short fable (story) was a famous American writer of gently humorous stories. He frequently drew illustrations for the stories he wrote. In fact, he is equally known for his work as a cartoonist.

   Thurber drew illustrations that looked like the moth and (bridge) lamp shown here.

B. Vocabulary Awareness—Learn the meaning of these **key expressions:**
The following three verbs are almost synonymous—they all refer to the result of strong heat or fire:
   1. to burn/cause a burn—is to be completely or partly consumed by the act of burning
      Example: *The oil wells burned for many hours.*
   2. to singe/cause a singe—is to burn only superficially, mostly at the edges
      Example: *Her long hair was slightly singed by the fire.*
   3. to scorch/to become scorched—is to become dried up or parched as a result of strong heat or fire
      Example: *The earth was scorched by the hot sun.*

The Moth and the Star

by James Thurber

A young and impressionable moth once set his heart on a certain star. He told his mother about this and she counselled him to set his heart on a bridge lamp instead. "Stars aren't the thing to hang around," she said; "lamps are the thing to hang around." "You get somewhere that way," said the moth's father. "You don't get anywhere chasing stars." But the moth would not heed the words of either parent. Every evening at dusk when the star came out he would start flying toward it and every morning at dawn he would crawl back home worn out with his vain endeavor. One day his father said to him, "You haven't burned a wing in months, boy, and it looks to me as if you were never going to. All your brothers have been badly burned flying around street lamps and all your sisters have been terribly singed flying around house lamps. Come on, now, get out of here and get yourself scorched! A big strapping moth like you without a mark on him!"

The moth left his father's house, but he would not fly around street lamps and he would not fly around house lamps. He went right on trying to reach the star, which was four and one-third light years, or twenty-five trillion miles, away. The moth thought it was just caught in the top branches of an elm. He never did reach the star, but he went right on trying, night after night, and when he was a very, very old moth he began to think that he really had reached the star and he went around saying so. This gave him a deep and lasting pleasure, and he lived to a great old age. His parents and his brothers and his sisters had all been burned to death when they were quite young.

Moral: Who flies afar from the sphere of our sorrow is here today and here tomorrow.

heed—pay attention to
vain endeavour—an effort that gives no results

Post-Reading Activities

A. You read the story by James Thurber not for information but rather to add to your background knowledge on the theme of individual versus group responsibilities.

Discuss these questions with a partner or in a small group:

1. Do you know anyone whose personality and outlook are similar to those of the moth described by Thurber?
2. How would you describe your own personality and outlook? Are you similar to Thurber's moth?
3. Do you know any fathers who are similar to the one described in the story?
4. How would you describe your own father?

B. James Thurber wrote many short stories. One you might enjoy reading is "The Secret Life of Walter Mitty."

Fourth Selection
Are You An Achiever?

Pre-Reading Tactics

This self-examination, taken from a popular magazine, asks questions to help you find out if you are a practical or impractical person. Since the purpose of reading this self-examination is primarily for enjoyment, have fun with it.

Try working with a partner. One person is the interviewer who asks the questions and writes the letter (a, b, c) of the reply. The other is the person who is interviewed.

Questionnaire

by Frank Donegan

Some of the questions ask you to make subjective judgments about your skills and attitudes. This is not easy to do, but if you want an accurate evaluation of whether you take a practical or impractical approach to life, give it a good try.

1. Are your political beliefs:
   a. Extremely left-wing.
   b. Quite liberal.
   c. Middle-of-the-road.
   d. Quite conservative.
2. How well do you handle your finances?
   a. Terribly. I always overspend and take on debts I can't afford.
   b. Fairly well. I live within my means.
   c. I'm extremely careful about my finances.
3. Do you feel you have a strong need to exercise power?
   a. Yes, being in a position to take advantage of people is a great feeling.
   b. Yes, I find it exhilarating to exercise authority.
   c. No, striving for power doesn't interest me.
4. Are you goal-oriented?
   a. Yes, once I set my mind on a goal, I'll sacrifice anything to get it.
   b. No.
   c. Yes, but I can substitute one goal for another.
5. If you had a spare $2,000 at the end of the year, would you be more likely to:
   a. put it into an investment.
   b. take a trip.
6. Are you the type of person who often jumps to conclusions?
   a. Yes.
   b. No, I believe judgments should be made on the basis of fact, not emotion.
7. If you have a number of different tasks to do, how do you usually approach them?
   a. I like to finish one task completely before I go to the next.
   b. I like to work on several things at once.

8. Do you prefer:
   a. to work as part of a team
   b. to work at something that allows you to be on your own.
9. Which of the following strategies are you more likely to use?
   a. As a salesman, it's important to be equally aggressive with every prospect.
   b. Save your energy for the people who are interested in what you have to sell.
10. Let's say you're married. You get along well with your husband/ wife in virtually all respects, but sex has become boring. Which of the following would you be most likely to do?
    a. I'd get a divorce.
    b. I'd begin looking around for a man/woman who could satisfy my needs.
    c. I'd probably stay married but would certainly look for a man/ woman with whom I could easily have a discreet affair.
    d. I'd stay married and wouldn't try to play around on the side.
11. Do you hold grudges for a long time?
    a. Yes.
    b. Sometimes.
    c. Not usually.
12. Do you take spur-of-the-moment vacations?
    a. Yes.
    b. Occasionally.
    c. No.
13. Do you regularly spend more than $5 a week on any sort of gambling?
    a. Yes.
    b. No, but I'm not opposed to gambling occasionally for fun.
    c. Never gamble under any circumstances.
14. How do you feel about fate?
    a. Fate is the dominant force that shapes destinies.
    b. Fate, chance, and luck exist, but we can cushion against bad luck and cash in on good luck.
    c. We make our own luck. "Fate" is basically an excuse made up by people who haven't planned properly.
15. Would you be more likely to agree or disagree with this statement: "People who are well-paid for their work should not complain if it is difficult or boring. Work isn't supposed to be a vacation."
    a. Agree
    b. Disagree ▶

Questionnaire—cont'd

16. You have to give a presentation before a large group of important people. Would you:
    a. Write out exactly what you wanted to say and read it to the audience.
    b. Thoroughly prepare what you wanted to say beforehand, but use only a few notes during the presentation.
    c. Just get up and talk.

17. How do you feel about making speeches in public?
    a. I love it.
    b. I don't relish the idea, but I do it when necessary.
    c. I hate making speeches and will do anything to avoid it.

18. Do you like to argue?
    a. Yes, arguing is a form of sport.
    b. I feel that I can convince others of the correctness of my views.
    c. No, arguing is a waste of time.

19. Do you have the type of personality that can delegate responsibility?
    a. Yes.
    b. Yes, in small matters.
    c. No; to get something done right, you have to do it yourself.

20. If money were no object, what kind of automobile would you own?
    a. I'd get the most economical and dependable one I could find.
    b. I would buy an expensive but "sensible" car.
    c. I'd like an exotic, unusual car.

Scoring

All possible answers have been awarded point values, which are listed below. To find your score, add up the point values of the answers you have chosen. The highest score is 100 points; the lowest, 20.

1. a–1, b–4, c–5, d–3, e–1
2. a–1, b–5, c–1
3. a–3, b–5, c–1
4. a–3, b–1, c–5
5. a–5, b–1
6. a–1, b–3, c–5
7. a–1, b–5
8. a–5, b–1
9. a–1, b–5
10. a–1, b–5, c–5, d–3
11. a–1, b–5, c–5
12. a–1, b–5, c–3
13. a–1, b–5, c–3
14. a–1, b–5, c–3
15. a–1, b–5
16. a–3, b–5, c–1
17. a–1, b–5, c–3
18. a–1, b–5, c–3
19. a–5, b–3, c–1
20. a–3, b–5, c–1

If you scored 74 to 100 points: You have true practical intelligence. You seek out the most efficient way to achieve the end you want. You use money wisely. You make plans and set objectives but remain flexible enough to change them.

47 to 73 points: Other people probably consider you extremely practical. When given choices, you select the most obviously "practical" alternative. Yet you seem to lack the flexibility and vision that characterize people who scored in the category above you. You're almost too practical for your own good. You're so intent on working toward short-term goals that you may be overlooking the opportunities that can bring you long-term success. However, your natural practicality may enable you to achieve some striking things.

20 to 46 points: You appear to be wildly impractical, and you're probably happy to be that way since practical people are likely to bore you. Getting places punctually, paying your rent on time, and keeping your wardrobe up to date may sometimes be completely beyond you. Yet it's from the ranks of people like you that the great scientific and artistic visionaries often emerge.

Unit Three
Getting Wheels . . .

Background Information for Unit Three

Buying a car is a luxury for some people, a purchase they cannot imagine making. For many, however, having a car is necessary for commuting—to get to work or to school. If you are thinking of buying a new or used car, you should do your homework first by collecting information about car buying through reading. When you finish Unit Three, you will know a great deal about how to select a car . . . you will know how to shop for wheels.

Selection One gives advice to new car shoppers. Since a car is one of the largest purchases most of us make, it pays to know what to look for. In fact, there are many sources to read which give information about cars. Some of them are listed in Selection One, ''How to Buy a New Car.'' Selecting a new car involves making choices. Sylvia Porter, the author of Selection One, carefully outlines what these choices are.

The buyer of a secondhand car needs even more specialized knowledge, the kind of information presented in Selection Two, ''How to Check Out a Used Car.'' Depending on your purpose for reading it, you may decide to overlook the details and just skim the article for the main ideas. Following it, you will read classified ads for secondhand cars from a newspaper—the best place to look if you're in the market for a used car.

There are other ways to look at getting wheels—for example, by considering how the automobile affects our lifestyles, our cities, and our total environment. In Selection Four, Tony Jones discusses cars from this critical perspective. The dilemma, as he sees it, is that we cannot live with or without our autos.

How to Buy a New Car

Pre-Reading Tactics

A. This slightly edited selection is taken from a popular "how to" book about personal money managing. The writing in "how to" books is clear and concise. The reader wants to find the information quickly; after all, "time is money."

B. The book contains practical information on everyday matters such as budgets, inflation, and financing an education. Sylvia Porter, the author, has also written many newspaper and magazine articles about personal finances.
If you plan to buy a car, then, you will want to read the article carefully. If you are not in the market for a car, remember: most of us sooner or later seem to need one.

C. As you read, think about the author's question (No. 5):
Do you believe social status (standing/ranking) is expressed by the kind of car one owns?

D. Vocabulary Awareness—Learn these **key expressions** by matching each one with the best meaning:

Key Expressions	**Meanings**
1. in the market for	_____ the loss in value of a car over time
2. depreciation	_____ possible choices
3. accessories	_____ looking in order to buy
4. options	_____ a price which is OK for both buyer/seller
5. a fair deal	_____ additions to a car after it leaves the factory

You can read the selection *without* using a dictionary. Try it!

How to Buy a New Car

by Sylvia Porter

You are in the market for a *new* car. How do you choose a reliable car dealer? When is the best time of the year to buy? Which accessories are worth the extra cost? How can you tell whether or not you are getting a fair deal if you're trading in your old car?

TEN BASIC GUIDES

1   (1) In advance, set a maximum price you are willing and able to pay for the car—everything included.

If you are a family with average income and expenses, plan to hold your monthly payments on a car you are buying over a period of three and a half to four years to one half or less of your monthly housing costs (mortgage and taxes *or* rent).

But, more important: what will your carrying costs be—your monthly payments *plus* your other fixed and monthly car costs—exclusive of depreciation?

2   (2) Also in advance, decide in some detail what *kind* of car you want.

This includes make, size, body type, engine, transmission. Will the size you choose meet your actual family needs, including those of growing children? Are you looking for an all-purpose family first car? Or one mainly for your job? Or primarily for long trips? Or just to go back and forth from the railroad station? What kind of weather will you be driving in? In what kind of traffic conditions? How much cargo room do you regularly need—honestly? (Roof racks or rented trailers are more economical for very occasional cargo hauling than an investment in a station wagon.)

3   (3) Do your homework before you buy.

Among your best sources are: the "Annual Roundup for New Car Buyers" issue of *Consumer Reports,* which includes frequency-of-repair records for popular makes and models, published in April and available at newsstands; the yearly "Buying Guide" issue of *Consumer Reports,* published in December and available at newsstands or from Consumers Union of U.S., Inc., 256 Washington Street, Mount Vernon, New York 10550; Edmund's *New Car Prices* (American makes) or *Foreign Car Prices,* from Edmund Publications Corporation, 515 Hempstead Turnpike, West Hempstead, New York 11552; Car/Puter's *New Car Yearbook,* from Davis Publications, Inc., 300 Lexington Avenue, New York, New York 10017; such auto and motor journals as *Car & Driver, Road and Track, Motor Trend, Automotive News,* which compare performance, price, and other aspects of each new model. (Check current prices for each publication.) Ford Motor Company publishes *Car Buying Made Easier,* which is full of easily understandable information on car buying. For a free copy, write: Ford Motor Company Listens, The American Road, Dearborn, Michigan 48121. (The box number usually is the year in which you write.)

4   (4) Use the following abbreviated chart to rate various new cars you are considering buying and to compare costs:

	Car 1	Car 2	Car 3
Net cash price:	_____	_____	_____
Taxes:	_____	_____	_____
Preparation costs:	_____	_____	_____
Cost of other extras:	_____	_____	_____
Cost of options you want:	_____	_____	_____
Key warranty coverage:			
Miles	_____	_____	_____
Years	_____	_____	_____
Parts	_____	_____	_____
Labor	_____	_____	_____
Other	_____	_____	_____
Expected gas mileage:	_____	_____	_____
Safety features:			
Passing ability	_____	_____	_____
Stopping distance	_____	_____	_____
Tire reserve load	_____	_____	_____
Space:	_____	_____	_____
Ride:	_____	_____	_____
Frequency-of-repair record:	_____	_____	_____
Handling:	_____	_____	_____
Luggage space:	_____	_____	_____
Passenger space:	_____	_____	_____
Ease of getting in and out:	_____	_____	_____
Looks:	_____	_____	_____
Dealer's reputation:	_____	_____	_____
Availability of parts, service:	_____	_____	_____
Efficiency of service:	_____	_____	_____

5   (5) Be honest with yourself about how important status is to you, as expressed by an automobile.

6   (6) Ask yourself how long you intend to keep the car. The longer you keep the car, the lower its cost will be, since depreciation is greatest in the earlier years.

7   (7) All other things being equal, buy a car which a dealer has in stock. Obviously, color, options, two-door, four-door styles, plus make and size ▶

How to Buy a New Car—cont'd

are important considerations; but be prepared to bend one way or another, or be ready to shop several dealers *in your own area* for one which has in stock a vehicle acceptable to you. The dealer is paying interest on *his* purchase of that car, too, and wants to unload it. And his markup margin on options may be two to three times his profit margin on cars.

8　(8) Make up your mind in advance and in the quiet of your own home what options are really important to you. Typically, purchased accessories can add one third or more to the total list price of your car. Consider choosing a car in stock which may be minus what you think is a key item. You always can purchase most options from discount stores and install them yourself.

9　(9) Consider the *gasoline mileage*—and other maintenance costs—of the car. But don't overstress such aspects. You can get a *relative* idea of what mileage you'll achieve by looking at the stickers on the car windows, but that is about all.

　　The mileage you really attain depends upon so many factors that it is impossible to make these comparisons properly.

Post-Reading Activities

A. Work with a partner:

Scan the article, then take turns giving each other advice on how to buy a new car. The clues below will help you locate the information as you **scan:**

1. What should you *decide on* before making a purchase?
2. What should you *do* before making a purchase?
3. What should you *consider* before making a purchase?

B. Do you have a friend or relative who is planning to buy a new car? Give him/her the rating chart on page 39. Find out if the chart helped that person decide on which car to purchase.

How to Check Out a Used Car

Pre-Reading Tactics

A. Although it is written for a general audience, this article gives detailed information. If you're not a car buff (enthusiast), you probably want to read it only for the main ideas, not the details. As you read, look for two kinds of suggestions:
1. General recommendations for buying a new car.
2. Recommendations about how to check out specific parts of a car.

B. Notice the by-line. (The ''by-line'' gives the name of the writer. Magazine articles and newspaper features usually have a by-line.) Can you guess why the article was written by a woman? What is a handywoman?

C. Vocabulary Awareness—Learn the meaning of these **key expressions:**
market value
test-drive
secondhand car

The _____ _____ of a used car is the price that one is likely to get for it. Before we buy a _____, we need to examine it and make sure that it works well. It is customary to _____-_____ a used car before buying.

You can understand the main ideas of the selection without using your dictionary for other unknown words. Try it!

How to Check Out a Used Car

HOW TO FIND A CREAM PUFF, PICK A PEACH AND STEER CLEAR OF THE LEMONS

Finding a good secondhand car can be tricky, but some thorough research can at least eliminate the real lemons. In general, the best used cars are between two and four years old, with 15,000 to 25,000 miles on them. And since the cost of gasoline has forced many big-car owners *to opt* for compact models, you may get a better price if you are willing to buy a larger car.

For a listing on the current market value of used cars, check the *Official Used Car Guide,* available at most banks and finance companies. (This publication is known simply as the "blue book" and is put out by the National Automobile Dealers' Association.)

Here are some other buying tips:

1. It is always best to inspect the car during daylight hours. Otherwise, it is easy to miss some telltale flaws, such as a rippling of the metal on the hood or slight color differences on the body panels. (Both are signs that the car has had some body work done, possibly as the result of *rust* or a *collision*.)

2. Check the appearance of the car's interior against the odometer reading. If the seats sag and the carpet is threadbare, don't believe an odometer that reads only 10,000 miles. (The numbers on the odometer should read perfectly straight across; if they do not, they may have been illegally tampered with.)

3. Examine all the tires. If the tire-wear indicators (the strips set into the tire tread, which appear when there is only 1/16 inch of tread left) are visible, the tires will soon have to be replaced. Be wary of tires that are worn on one edge only; uneven wear could simply mean that the wheels need to be realigned, but it could also indicate sagging springs, worn ball joints or deterioration of any of the components that connect the wheel to the car.

4. A rust-proofed car is worth the additional money, especially if you live near salt water or in an area where the roads are heavily salted in winter. The main spots to check for rust: around the wheel wells, the bottoms of the doors, under the floor mats and on the underside of the car. If you can poke a pencil through any rust spots, look for another car.

5. Check underneath the car for leaks. Any leak, other than water from the air conditioner, signals trouble.

6. Unless the oil has been changed very recently, it will probably be black. Oil that is a milky-brown color has become contaminated with coolant and means a possible head-gasket leak.

Be sure there are no dirt particles or silver-gray metal deposits clinging to the oil dipstick, and that no water has seeped into the tank (any water will be floating on top). The same goes for the transmission fluid. (After you have driven the car, check the transmission fluid again to make sure there is no scorched smell, which could mean that the transmission system needs overhauling.)

7. Bounce each corner of the car. Good *shocks* should bounce only once.

8. Start the engine. It should turn over within a few seconds and run smoothly without coughing or sputtering. There should be no smoke coming from the exhaust (blue smoke indicates that the engine is burning oil; black smoke means the car probably needs a tune-up).

9. Be sure the window buttons, seat-adjustment levers, heater, trunk lock, and so forth, are in working order.

10. Test-drive the car both on the highway and in stop-and-go traffic. Does it accelerate smoothly and switch gears easily? If you take your hands off the steering wheel, does the car continue straight ahead? (If it veers, the wheel bearings may be loose or the wheels may need realigning.) Is the steering mechanism firm, the wheel easy to control? (If there is a lot of play in the wheel, the wheel bearings could be loose or the ball joints worn.) When the car is idling, are you able to use the air conditioner, lights and radio simultaneously, without stalling? (If not, the battery is probably low.)

11. Take any car you are seriously considering to a mechanic you trust or to an auto diagnostic clinic (check prices beforehand). Ask the mechanic about any strange noises, vibrations or smells you noticed while driving. After his inspection, which should include a test drive, he should be able to tell you the general condition of the car and what components will soon need replacement or repair.

12. Be sure to get any agreement in writing, even if you are dealing with a private owner.

13. Don't be afraid to *dicker over* price: By now, you should know whether the asking price is fair. You'll be better off selling your old car privately, since you'll never be given the full market value on a trade-in.

---

to opt—to select
rust—deterioration of metal
collision—an auto accident
shocks—short word for shock absorbers
to dicker over—to bargain
check out—to find out about something
a lemon—a car, new or used, that never works well

Post-Reading Activities

A. Use the information from the article! Suppose you wanted to have a summary of the information in the article to take along when you shop for a used car. The article lists eight *parts* of a car that need to be checked out.

Scan the article to find five of them. Write a key expression that would help you remember the part of the car and what to look for.

Example: *trunk lock—working order*

1. _____

2. _____

3. _____

4. _____

5. _____

B. Scan the article to find five *general recommendations* for buying a used car.

Write key expressions that will help you shop for a used car.

1. _____

2. _____

3. _____

4. _____

5. _____

C. Find the **compounds:**

Many concepts in English are made up of two or three nouns. Together they form a compound which takes on a new meaning. In this selection there are many such compounds.

Find the compounds that have the same meaning as the expressions given below.

1. Cars that don't get rusty are _____

2. A leak from the head-gasket is a _____

3. Traffic that stops often is _____

4. Indicators that can tell you how worn out the tires are

_____

5. Levers that enable seat adjusting are _____

Classified Ads: Used Cars

Pre-Reading Tactics

Read the ads below. Think about your needs as a car purchaser. If you're not in the market for a car now, imagine you have just moved to a city where it is necessary to commute to work or school. So, you'll need to have a car. Which car advertised below would you want to check out?

1 '80 CHEV CITATION, 4 dr, hatchback, 6 cyl, auto, a/c, extras. Exc. cond., 1 owner. 78,000 mi. $3100 OBO. Harriet, 742-6384.	**5 '80 TOYOTA TERCEL,** 2dr, 4spd, 51k mi, new ($1200) engine, v.g. cond, yellow. $2850. Owner leaving USA. 207-4730.
2 1979 DATSUN 210 Hatchback, stick, air. Great gas mileage. $2300. 742-8206 days, 695-4914 eves.	**6 ALFA ROMEO** 1978 Spider, red/tan top, AM/FM cass, 80k miles, xlnt cond, 1 owner, $4950 (RMBLNGY). 748-8262 day, ask for Mark.
3 '74 FIREBIRD FORMULA 400, ram air, 4 spd, a/c, mags. $1500 OBO. 734-9595.	**7 1983 BMW 635CSI,** 5 sp, loaded. Anthracite blk lthr interior. US specs. Must sell. Best offer over $22,000. Call evenings. 204-2359.
4 '82 TOYOTA SUPRA fully equipped, 46k, white. Must sell, excellent cond. $2800 down, take over $6000 pmt. 671-5739.	

Post-Reading Activities

A. Read the ads to answer these questions. (Use the numbers in front of the ads.)

   1. Which is the newest car advertised? _____

   2. Which is the oldest? _____

   3. Which is the most expensive? _____

   4. Which is the cheapest? _____

   5. In which case do you think you could dicker over price? _____

B. Find the classified ad section in your city's newspaper. Use the questions in A to practice reading classified ads more easily.

Living With/Without an Automobile

Pre-Reading Tactics

A. This article first appeared in *Harper's,* a magazine of opinions and ideas. For more than a hundred years, this magazine has been edited for readers who expect to be entertained and intellectually challenged by its writings. The version you will read has been shortened somewhat.

B. Vocabulary Awareness—Learn the **key expressions:**
By understanding the first sentence, you will be able to grasp one of the author's main points.

The paradox the automobile has thrust upon us is that liberation is bondage.

liberation (freedom)   bondage (slavery)
liberate   bond
liberator
So, the automobile gives us freedom but also enslaves us. A *paradox,* then, means a statement which is true/false (choose one) yet at the same time seems contradictory.

C. You may find quite a few unknown words in this article. In the first reading, try to find the overall meaning. Circle the words you don't know, but keep on reading. Then, use the exercise in **Post-Reading Activities** to practice guessing the meaning of words from context clues when possible.

Living With/Without an Automobile

by Tony Jones

1 The paradox the automobile has thrust upon us is that liberation is bondage. The automobile has made it possible, literally and figuratively, to go anywhere, to be anyone. The most important freedom has become the freedom to move—to a new town, a new part of the country, a new life. The car has provided a fast, efficient, adaptable, identifiable engine of forward (and upward) mobility, and as such it became an important cultural symbol system, a language practically everyone spoke. In some dimension it represented mastery over the *truculence* of the natural world.

2 Today, the automobile is mostly thought of as a necessity. Outside the cities it is hard to the point of impossibility to discharge the business of daily living without its help. Jobs, vacations, friendships, family ties—all seem to depend on the reach provided by the car. It is the needle by which we have learned to sew together the pieces of our lives, and without it our image of ourselves is *tatterdemalion*. For all its small *tyrannies,* the car is still a cornerstone of life, a convenience so taken for granted that its absence in our individual lives is almost beyond comprehension.

3 However logical and rational these judgments of personal necessity, when they are multiplied one hundred million times (the number of cars in the land) the result is social insanity. At that scale, the sheer force of the automobile's presence commands that we be willing to sacrifice most other needs to its priority. As a collective entity, the automobile threatens to make us its servant. It requires that we plan our cities (or dig them up and rebuild them) around its needs, on pain of death by choking; that we flatten the landscape before it, in the service of speed and directness; that we make unprecedented demands on our natural resources, in the name of economic necessity. We are awakening to the way the automobile has dominated the national business of law enforcement, has concentrated staggering economic power in the auto industries, has reduced us to the barbarity of one driver shooting another over a parking space—a contemporary image that suggests the automobile's impact on our assumptions about community. Most immediately, it is poisoning the air around us, while experts dispute the rate at which we are approaching the intolerable. ▶

truculence—harsh, cruel
tatterdemalion—a person in torn, ragged clothing
tyrannies—unfair, abusive use of power

Living With/Without an Automobile—cont'd

4   Overall, it's a standoff. The car has assumed the confusing status of something we can't live with, can't live without.

5   The trouble with most schemes to deal with the problems created by the automobile is that they underestimate the vastness of their undertaking. The car serves a variety of needs other than transportation and, for all its concrete reality, its greatest powers may be symbolic.

6   The automobile provides privacy. Next to the bathroom, it is the nicest, easiest, most acceptable place to be alone. People sing, scream, pick their noses, talk to the radio, and do all manner of other odd and private things within the isolation of their cars. Surely the vast queues of commuters, one to a car, would not suffer their daily bumper-to-bumper indignities if there weren't something pleasurable about being alone in a car.

7   The automobile allows an exercise of power. Driving represents a challenge to be overcome; there is a constant parade of tiny decisions that await your action and that certify you as skilled and needed— the master of your ship. It makes perfect sense, therefore, that getting a driver's license has become the rite of passage to the adult world. If you drive, you are competent, responsible, powerful, your own man.

8   The automobile magnifies the sense of spontaneity in life. A decision involving travel can be made instantaneously if a car is available. Thus spontaneity becomes a proof of freedom: there's no requirement to be bound by schedules of any sort, and the car becomes the ideal transmitter of impulse. As Detroit well knows, buying a particular car is frequently an impulsive decision— logically enough, since the car it-

self stands for the glorification of impulse.

9   Above all, the automobile is an instrument of choice. Selecting a car is like facing a keyboard and being asked to pick out an individual melody. Or, if you like, it's like choosing a face to put on for the world. We think of cars as possessing personalities, so they become, to a greater or lesser extent, externalizations of our value systems. A Volkswagen has a different cachet from a Pontiac GTO, a Lincoln speaks in a voice different from a Ford's. Because it is practically *ubiquitous*, the car be-

10   comes a badge of identification and is quite knowingly worn as such. Even those who renounce a car are making a statement with the same symbolic language.

Because the automobile trails such a variety of other associations, the attempts to deal with it strictly as a transportation tool miss the mark. They can win minor readjustments in the *status quo*, but they have little hope of affecting the overall patterns of usage that constitute the affliction. It's the kind of problem that legislation can affect but cannot solve.

ubiquitous—present everywhere

status quo—the state in which things are now (implies: no change will be made in the way things are now)

Post-Reading Activities

A. Use the clues in the context of the paragraph to help guess the meaning of these words:

1. Paragraph 3
Social insanity means:
clue: a hundred million times
a. an individual is insane.
b. the whole society is insane.
c. I'm okay; you're okay.

2. Paragraph 4
A standoff means:
clue: we can't live with/without cars
a. the result is a tie.
b. a decision can be made.
c. a decision is not necessary.

3. Paragraph 6

A queue is:

clue: cars . . . bumper-to-bumper

a. being alone in a car.

b. cars in a collision.

c. cars/people in a line.

4. A rite of passage means:

clue: getting a driver's license . . . the adult world

a. applying for a driver's license.

b. the formal ceremony of becoming adult.

c. a birthday celebration.

5. A cachet means:

clue: it's like choosing a face to put on

a. a distinguishing mark.

b. a color.

c. a style.

B. Be ready to discuss these questions in a small group. How many arguments can you find in the article which support each of these views:

Pro-Cars	Con-Cars
The auto has made it possible to go anywhere, to be anyone.	*The sheer force of the automobile's presence commands that we sacrifice most other needs to its priority.*
_____	_____
_____	_____
_____	_____
_____	_____

C. In paragraphs 4 and 5, the author states his main points. What are they?

_____   _____

D. Do you agree with him that automobiles are symbols for other values?

E. According to the author, what do automobiles represent for us, symbolically speaking? (paragraphs 6, 7, 8, 9)

F. Can you live without a car? Do you know others who do? In what cities is it possible to live without a car?

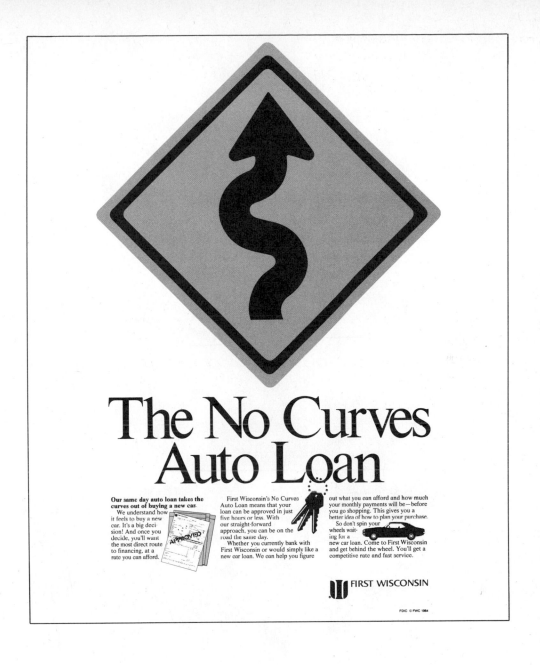

The No Curves Auto Loan

Our same day auto loan takes the curves out of buying a new car.

We understand how it feels to buy a new car. It's a big decision! And once you decide, you'll want the most direct route to financing, at a rate you can afford.

First Wisconsin's No Curves Auto Loan means that your loan can be approved in just five hours or less. With our straight-forward approach, you can be on the road the same day.

Whether you currently bank with First Wisconsin or would simply like a new car loan. We can help you figure out what you can afford and how much your monthly payments will be—before you go shopping. This gives you a better idea of how to plan your purchase.

So don't spin your wheels waiting for a new car loan. Come to First Wisconsin and get behind the wheel. You'll get a competitive rate and fast service.

FIRST WISCONSIN

FDIC © FWC 1984

G. This ad plays with words and symbols.
  1. Do you recognize the road sign? It is used world-wide.
  2. What product is the ad selling?
  3. Would you select an auto loan called ''No Curves?''

... On Credit

Background Information for Unit Four

More and more people are attracted to the idea of buying on credit and using credit cards. Having a credit card enables you to carry very little cash, a consideration in big cities where people think about security. Buying on credit also makes it possible to spread the payments over a period of time; of course, there is the added cost of interest payments. But the most attractive yet dangerous aspect of the credit system is that you can buy things even if, at the moment, you haven't the money.

Although the credit card system makes for easier shopping and managing of money, there is an important feature which is often ignored by unwise credit card users. With a credit card you have to handle your expenses far more carefully than if you only used cash. In order not to get into debt over your head, you must keep an account of what you will have to pay. Unfortunately, many credit card users fall into the trap of "spending now and worrying about it later."

Of the four selections in this unit, each deals with a different aspect of credit buying. The first is a form to fill out to apply for credit with a department store. Selection II gives some important tips for protecting yourself if you are a credit card user. Then, in Selection III, you will read in-depth about how credit cards came into use. The article makes us realize that intricately tied to credit cards is the word "plastic" (in informal English it means to pay with a credit card) as well as the computer. Without both, the credit system as it exists today could not work. Then, Selection IV offers further information on how to manage your personal financial affairs in a world that runs on credit.

Application for Credit

Pre-Reading Tactics

A. Find the **objective:**

This application is for customers who want to be able to charge their purchases in a department store. They want to buy now, pay later. Credit, if approved, will be given by the store. What information do you think the store might want about the applicant? To check your guess, read the subtitles printed in boldface boxes on the application. List the six subtitles below:

_____   _____

_____   _____

_____   _____

B. Fill in the application as if you were going to apply for credit at the store. Notice that this application can be filled in by two people, an applicant and a joint-applicant. If you care to, you and a partner can fill in the application together.

C. Vocabulary Awareness—Use these key expressions in the paragraph below.

individual account   one (user)   co-applicant
joint account   two (users)

If you work with a partner, you will apply for a _____ _____.

Your partner is the _____. If you fill out the application alone, you will

apply for an _____ _____. An individual account can have _____or

_____users.

CREDIT APPLICATION

LITTLES'

TYPE ACCOUNT (CHECK ONE)
☐ OPTION ACCOUNT   ☐ INSTALLMENT ACCOUNT
(INSTALLMENT ACCOUNTS ARE FOR LARGE PURCHASES)

NAME ADDRESS

(CHECK ONE)
☐ JOINT ACCOUNT
☐ INDIVIDUAL ACCOUNT

(CHECK ONE)
☐ ONE USER
☐ TWO USERS

(CHECK ONE)
☐ OWN   ☐ RENT
☐ LIVE WITH PARENTS

Name

Name-Co–Applicant

Street Address

Apartment-Suite   (Area) Home Phone ( ) —

City   State   Zip   How Long Yrs. Mos.

PREVIOUS ADDRESS

Previous Address (if less than 2 years) Street

City   State   Zip   How Long Yrs. Mos.

CREDIT REFERENCE

Name And Branch of Bank   ☐ Checking   ☐ Savings   Credit Reference

Credit Reference   Credit Reference

Have You Ever Had An Account With Us   Account Number
☐ Yes   ☐ No

Nearest Relative Not Living With You   Address

APPLICANT

Social Security No. — —   Birth Date   Income   ☐ Wk ☐ Mo ☐ Yr

You need not disclose income from alimony, child support or maintenance payments unless you wish such income considered for credit.   OTHER INCOME ANNUAL AMOUNT   SOURCE

Employed By (Firm Name)   How Long Yrs. Mos.

Business Address

Position   (Area) Business Phone ( ) —

Previous Employer (If Less Than 1 Year)

Previous Position   How Long Yrs. Mos.

JOINT-APPLICANT

Social Security No. — —   Birth Date   Income   ☐ Wk ☐ Mo ☐ Yr

You need not disclose income from alimony, child support or maintenance payments unless you wish such income considered for credit.   OTHER INCOME ANNUAL AMOUNT   SOURCE

Employed By (Firm Name)   How Long Yrs. Mos.

Position   (Area) Business Phone ( ) —

(Area) Phone ( ) —

Post-Reading Activities

A. Understand the information required:

1. Under the subtitle *Name–Address*, what other information must the applicant give?
   a. Why ask *own/rent/live with parents?*
   b. Why ask *how long?*
2. Why does the store want a *previous address?*
3. How many *credit references* is the applicant asked to give?

4. Why would an applicant select not to give information about income from alimony, child support, or maintenance payments?

5. Is the *joint-applicant* assumed to be financially responsible? How do you know?

6. What legal rights does the applicant/buyer have? Where are they explained on the application form?

B. Collect some other applications for credit—for example, American Express credit cards, Mastercards, VISA. Bring the applications to class. Do these other types of creditors ask applicants for information that differs from the questions the department store asks?

Second Selection
Dinner 'Deal' May Be Credit Card Trap

Pre-Reading Tactics

A. This short feature from a newspaper contains a letter seeking advice and a reply from a money management expert, Peter Weaver. The title in smaller print, "Mind Your Money," is used whenever the column appears; the title in larger print describes today's letter. Notice, it is written in newspaper headline style. What words have been left out? _____

B. Vocabulary Awareness:
The selection contains many expressions commonly used in informal, spoken English.
Match the meanings:

1. a "deal"	_____ to cost
2. to go for	_____ a price which is favorable for the buyer
3. drum up	_____ a hidden, unstated purpose
4. a catch to it	_____ to get people interested in
5. for real	_____ actually taking place

Mind Your Money

Dinner 'Deal' May Be Credit Card Trap

by Peter Weaver

1   **Question:** Someone called from a hotel and said we had been selected to receive restaurant dining privileges that allowed two dinners or lunches to go for the cost of one. To be put on the special listing, they needed our credit card number so the head waiter could identify us.

2   Is this a legitimate discount to drum up interest in the restaurant or is there a catch to it?

3   **Answer:** You should not have to give your credit card number over the phone. Too dangerous.

4   With your number, unscrupulous callers can then start charging goods through telephone orders for delivery elsewhere. Numbers can also be sold to crooks.

5   Have them put any offers in writing, and be sure to check out the place of business. Call the hotel management back and ask if this offer is for real. It probably isn't.

6   You should also be careful with your credit card number when you pay restaurant bills or make purchases. Keep the carbon with the receipt and destroy it.

7   One way to fend off credit card fraud is to carefully check your statement each month. Keep all your receipts and compare them with the stated charges.

8   Here's a checklist provided by American Express:

9   —Keep your card in view when a clerk takes it.

10   —If possible, avoid signing a blank receipt.

11   —Draw a line through blank spaces above the total.

12   —Carry cards separately from your wallet.

13   And, remember, if your cards are stolen or lost, phone in the facts immediately. Make sure you have the phone numbers for all your card creditors.

14   The law says once you report lost or stolen cards, your maximum liability is $50 per card. And most creditors waive the $50 penalty.

Post-Reading Activities

A. Guess meanings from the **context:**

Did you guess these meanings when you read the selection? Check your understanding of these words by filling in the missing letters:

1. Paragraphs 3, 4

Question: Why is it dangerous to give a credit card number over the telephone?

Answer: Because some un _____ callers are also c _____ .

2. Paragraph 7

Question: How can I f_____ off f_____?

Answer: If you don't want to be cheated, check your monthly statement carefully.

B. Understand the **information:**

1. The writer gives six recommendations for fending off credit card fraud. What are they?

_____   _____

_____   _____

_____   _____

2. Do you know what happens if credit cards are lost or stolen? With a partner, have a telephone conversation:

Speaker 1 (the customer):

"I lost my credit card. What should I do?"

Speaker 2 (the American Express representative):

_____

Be sure to change roles so each person has a chance to ask and answer the question.

Third Selection
Money Machines

Pre-Reading Tactics

A. This selection is part of a chapter taken from a nonfiction book titled *The Money Lenders*. Anthony Sampson, the author, has drawn on his background as a journalist to write books about global finance, multinational corporations, and the workings of international oil companies.

B. Understand the **organization:**

Use the organization of the material as an aid to understanding it.

1. The broader context from which the selection is taken is:

_____

2. What is the title of the chapter from which the selection is taken?

_____

3. The selection has two subtitles. What are they?

_____

_____

C. Understand the **style:**
1. The author frequently uses the past perfect tense. By doing so, he heightens the sense of historical perspective for the reader. His scope is broad across place and time.

time-line
Past perfect . . . . . past . . . . . present
      ↓   ↓

gives historical   the writer
perspective   is here

2. He also frequently uses *now* with past tense. This stylistic device also emphasizes the story-telling, narrative quality of the writing:

It was much harder now . . .

event-line
event 1. . . . . . . event 2 . . . . event 3 . . . . event (n)
               ↓   ↓   ↓

              now   now   now
              with respect
              to everything
              that happened
              before

D. At the beginning of the chapter there is quotation from a VISA advertisement. (VISA is the name of a bank credit card, similar to Mastercard and American Express.) Can you guess why the author selected it for this chapter?

E. What do you think a money machine is?

_____ a machine that makes money

_____ a machine that dispenses (gives out) money

As you read, ask yourself if the author had any other kind of machine in mind?

Read the selection without using your dictionary!

Money Machines

by Anthony Sampson

Anywhere you see our name is home
VISA advertisement

1   The style of a bank had changed since medieval money lenders counted coins on a bench, or the Italians lent gold to English kings. It was much harder now to trace the money from the beginning to the end—from the small saver leaving a few dollars in his local bank to the billion-dollar Eurodollar loans raised by a *syndicate* of two hundred banks to finance a country in the Far East. The banker who spent his time telephoning or traveling between New York and Tokyo had little in common with the teller who took dollar bills over the counter; the movements of billions of Eurodollars had long ago lost contact with any ordinary depositor, or even a government. The language of the global bankers—about financial services, corporate finance, recycling, rescheduling, or restructuring— suggested activities quite different from money lending for profit. Yet the business was still basically the same as the *Medicis'* or *Shylock's;* and the further the world went into debt, the more bankers prospered.

PLASTIC LOANS

2   The bankers had already discovered a new way to cross frontiers through the extraordinary development of the credit card, which was now providing still greater opportunities. It had begun modestly in February 1950, when the manager of a small loan company, Frank McNamara, established the Diners Club, which provided select members with credit at twenty-two restaurants in New York, and collected a commission in return for paying bills promptly. Then in 1958 American Express, which already had a world network through its tourist services and traveler's checks, began selling its green-and-white card as a prestigious *open-sesame* to hotels, restaurants, shops, and airlines all through America and across the world. The company made handsome profits from its charges (or ''discount rate'') to the shopowners or hoteliers, and from the cost of the card. It was not strictly a credit card, but a ''travel and entertainment'' (T&E) card: it insisted on its customers paying their bills within thirty days, after which it bombarded them with increasingly menacing computerized letters, culminating in angry telegrams and threats from its debt collectors. There were many bad debts and some spectacular

excesses—one Korean businessman built a whole apartment block on one card. But by 1980 American Express had about 10.5 million card holders across the world, far outstripping its rivals—Diners Club (4 million) and Carte Blanche (about 1.5 million)—both of which are now owned by Citicorp. American Express had already expanded into a major international bank, and it was now planning to offer a range of financial services direct to the home through new cable systems.

3   In the meantime the banks themselves were moving into credit cards. They were not so concerned with the charges to shops as with the interest they could collect if card holders did not pay promptly; while American Express threatened its wayward customers, the banks were much more relaxed and simply totted up the interest.

4   Visa and Mastercharge were now competing across the world, challenging the traditional territory of American Express. By 1979 Visa represented a network of 13,000 banks, including Barclays in Britain, the Carte Bleu group of 130 French banks, and a link with the Sumitomo Bank in Japan. In Germany Visa ran into fierce competition from the rival Eurocheque system with its own Eurocard, which in 1978 was bought up by a powerful European group headed by the Deutsche Bank. The Eurocard had forged its own links with Mastercharge in America and with the Access cards owned by a group of British banks. But Visa was more far-flung and versatile, offering bank loans as well as credit in shops or restaurants.

THE COMPUTER TRIUMPHS

5   It was a triumph for the computer. The huge Visa network of outlets and cardholders was run by only three hundred people, most of them in the headquarters outside San Francisco. The computers sorted out the millions of credits and debits and passed them on to the individual banks; the cost of a shirt bought in Milwaukee in the afternoon could be debited to an account in Barclays in Northamptom the next morning. The reminders of interest, the stern demands for payment were all chattered out by machines pretending to be people. The cards and computers allowed the bankers to lend money without ever having to see a customer or to employ an extra teller.   ▶

syndicate—a combination of bankers and other money lenders
Medicis—a rich, powerful medieval Italian family; early capitalists
Shylock—a money lender in Shakespeare's play *The Merchant of Venice*
open-sesame—a password at which gates open; from *The Arabian Nights*

Money Machines—cont'd

6   The controllers of this empire of credit cards had given great benefits to those citizens who were inside the system of credit, while automatically rejecting those who were not: the whole concept of trust which underlay credit had been taken over by machines. It was now marvelously easy for an individual to borrow and postpone repayment, but harder to make sure that he would have the money available.

7   The bankers still yearned for more automation, and they saw their credit cards as only one stage in the development of Electronic Funds Transfer (EFT), which could bypass people altogether with the help of an ATM (automatic teller machine), an OLTT (on-line teller terminal), and a POS (point-of-sale terminal). Their ambition was to build a system which would allow a customer to make his purchase through a point-of-sale terminal in a shop which would instantly debit his account in New York, or reject him if he had no money or credit. It was a thrilling prospect.

8   Nagging doubts still remained about the threat to the freedom of the individual. Already the credit card, when used for renting cars or hotel rooms, has proved an invaluable device for discreet surveillance by authoritarian governments like South Africa's which wish to keep track of people's movements without being seen to do so. Point-of-sale terminals, once linked up to a police computer, could tell the police where an individual was to be found at that very instant.

Post-Reading Activities

A. Check your understanding of the **main ideas:**

1. Paragraph 1

Over time, the activity of banking (choose one) _____ has changed

_____ has remained the same.

Old activities	*New activities*
Money lenders used to	Today, bankers
_____	_____
_____	_____
_____	_____

2. The further the world went into debt, the more bankers prospered. Is the situation the author describes a paradox?

_____Yes   _____ No

3. Plastic loans refer to

a. _____ certain people.

b. _____ small containers.

c. _____ credit cards.

4. What is the relationship between banks and the credit card business?

a. _____ Banks originated credit cards.

b. _____ Banks got into the credit card business.

c. _____ Banks were against credit cards.

5. Paragraph 5
". . . demands for payment were all chattered out by machines pretending to be people."
This refers to:

a. _____ computer printers.

b. _____ a roomful of noisy typists.

c. _____ 300 people who work for VISA.

6. Paragraph 6
The author does not explain what "to be inside the system of credit" means. Can you guess?

a. _____ to establish a credit rating

b. _____ to be denied credit

c. _____ to apply for credit

7. Paragraph 7
Why is automation a "thrilling prospect" to bankers? You must infer the answer:

a. _____ It advances technology.

b. _____ It increases the banks' business.

c. _____ It bypasses people.

8. The author points out that credit cards can be a threat to individual freedom.
   The implied meaning is that:
   a. _____ the computer can be used to keep track of people.

   b. _____ surveillance can be done by credit cards.

   c. _____ the account numbers on individual credit cards are stored in computers along with other information about the card-holders.

B. With a partner, compare your answers to Activity A.

C. Ask and tell each other: What are your experiences with the credit card system?

Fourth Selection

Credit Refused! Your Credit Rating Could Be Too Good!

Pre-Reading Tactics

A. Read the **title:**
   This selection from a popular magazine deals with customers being refused credit because their "credit is too good." What does this mean?

B. **Skim** the article, noting that certain words have been left out. Read it again, then fill in the appropriate words in the blanks. Only **one** word is allowed in each blank. In skimming, realize that you can understand the main ideas even though you are not reading every word!

C. Try to read the article a few sentences at a time to understand the overall meaning. This will help you fill in the blanks. Remember, you may think of more than one word which makes sense.

Credit Refused! Your Credit Rating Could Be Too Good!

by Barbara Gilder Quint

Many of us are routinely offered "lines of credit" of $1,000 or more by banks. Under these arrangements, you 1 _____ automatically overdraw your checking account or obtain cash against 2 _____ bank credit card, without filling out a formal loan 3 _____ . If you never use your line of credit, there 4 _____ no fee; if you do, you are charged interest 5 _____ the going rate.

On the surface, a line of 6 _____ looks like a no-lose deal: It's there if you 7 _____ it, but you don't pay if you don't use 8 _____ . As a result, it's tempting to accept another line 9 _____ one is offered. If you have several such credit 10 _____ , however, a problem can arise when you apply for 11 _____ new loan for a major purchase. The fact that 12 _____ have been granted all these credit lines will show up on your credit-bureau report. Even if you haven't used 13 _____ and don't plan to, a prospective lender may take 14 _____ into account in deciding whether to give you that 15 _____ loan. For example, the bank you've asked for the 16 _____ loan might agree that you currently would be able 17 _____ make the required payments. But they might question whether 18 _____ could afford your overall debt 19 _____ if, at some 20 _____ , you borrow against your credit lines to their maximum.

21 _____ on this reasoning, they could turn you down for 22 _____ car loan. Thus, it makes sense to limit the 23 _____ of credit lines you ▶

Credit Refused! Your Credit Rating Could Be Too Good—cont'd

accept, perhaps having only one. 24 _____ you are refused a loan because of "too much 25 _____ ," phone or write the credit bureau for a free 26 _____ of your credit report. If that's the case, ask 27 _____ bank(s) that granted the line(s) to reduce or eliminate them. 28 _____ , contact the lender who turned you down, explain what 29 _____ , and reapply for the loan.

Post-Reading Activities

A. Reread the passage to check if it makes sense.

B. With a partner or in a small group, compare the words you supplied for each blank. Sometimes a number of different words can be used which still maintain the meaning of the whole passage.

Finding Out About Our World: Popular Science

Background Information for Unit Five

The selections in this unit are linked together not only by an overall thematic connection but also by the type of writing which they represent. All three of these articles from newspapers and magazines present basic information about scientific topics to people who do not have specialized background in science. These readers want to find the facts stated clearly, briefly, and in a style that is easy to understand.

Isaac Asimov, the author of ''Back to Basics,'' is probably the best-known popular science writer in the world. The author of over 300 books and countless magazine articles, he is able to make complex subjects appealing and easy to read. Asimov tells about the advantages of using the basic material of rock. He describes how scientists concerned with conserving the earth's resources are trying to improve this material.

''Turtle May Be Clue . . .'' looks back in time by reporting on a recent scientific theory about dinosaurs, those creatures that lived on this planet millions of years ago and then disappeared. Next, ''4,000-Year Search . . .'' summarizes facts about a scientific question which people have faced for thousands of years: how to create accurate calendars that account for the movements of the sun, the moon, and the earth.

After reading all three selections, you should be able to suggest a theme they all share.

When you finish reading the three selections in Unit Five, turn back to this page. Write a new title for this unit which conveys what the three selections have in common. Write *your* title below.

Back to Basics

Pre-Reading Tactics

A. Look at the **title:**

Selection One, a typical Isaac Asimov popular science article, consists of 12 paragraphs. The title contains an appeal to the reader to "go back to something basic," but one cannot tell what the main theme is before reading the selection. **Skim** the first seven paragraphs, reading the first sentence in each. Notice what materials are mentioned in each paragraph. Can you now tell what "Back to Basics" might mean?

B. Find the **organization:**

The writer presents the reader with a main problem and then with a possible solution. Paragraphs 1 through 6 present the problem. As you read, try to formulate the problem for yourself. Paragraph 7 pinpoints the problem and offers a solution. The rest of the article raises some minor problems related to the suggested solution and offers ways to overcome these problems.

C. This article has an organization that is often found in scientific articles: problem—solution—evaluation of solution. Notice that the problem here is presented via a historical time line of the development of basic materials which we use in our daily lives. The author gives the readers facts and then draws our attention to some disadvantages which create the problem. The first words in each paragraph help us recognize whether the author is presenting facts or disadvantages:

Paragraph 1: *In prehistoric time* . . .
Paragraph 2: *But* . . .
Paragraph 3: *However,* . . .
Paragraph 4: *About 100 years ago* . . .
Paragraph 5: *In the Twentieth Century* . . .
Paragraph 6: *However,* . . .

As you read the article, pay special attention to how the author presents the facts and the disadvantages.

D. Vocabulary awareness—Learn the meaning of these **key expressions:**
Match an expression in A with a possible meaning in B:

A	B
1. resources	_____ does not change with age
2. (to be) extracted (from)	_____ form
3. mold (into shape)	_____ other ways
4. (ways of) treating (material)	_____ drawn, taken out
5. resistant to deterioration	_____ changing
6. (finding) alternatives	_____ sources of supply

E. Below is a photograph of a famous place in England called Stonehenge. People come from around the world to see these prehistoric rock formations. Isaac Asimov mentions Stonehenge in paragraph 1. Use an encyclopedia if you want to find more information about Stonehenge.

Back to Basics

by Isaac Asimov

1 In prehistoric times the chief toolmaking material was stone. In fact, that period is referred to as the Stone Age. There were advantages to stone: There was a lot of it. It could be had almost anywhere just for the picking up. And it lasted indefinitely. The pyramids still stand, and the rocks of Stonehenge are still there.

2 But then about 5,000 years ago, people began using metal. It had advantages. Whereas rock was *brittle* and had to be *chipped* into shape; metal was tough and could be beaten and bent into shape. Metal resisted a blow that would *shatter* rock, and metal held an edge when a stone edge would be *blunted*.

3 However, metal was much rarer than rock. Metal occasionally was found as nuggets, but generally it had to be extracted from certain not very common rocks (ores) by the use of heat. Finally, about 3,500 years ago, people found out how to extract iron from ores. Iron is particularly common metal and is the cheapest metal even today. Iron properly treated becomes steel, which is particularly hard and tough. However, iron and steel have a tendency to rust.

4 About 100 years ago aluminum came into use. It is a light metal and can be made even stronger than iron, pound for pound. What's more, it is even more common than iron and won't rust. However, aluminum holds on so tightly to the other atoms in its ores that a great deal of energy must be used to isolate it, so it is more expensive than iron.

5 In the Twentieth Century plastics came into use. They are light materials that are organic (that is, built of the same atoms that are found in living organisms). Plastics can be as tough as metals, can be molded into shape, can be resistant to water and to deterioration such as rust, and can come in all sorts of compositions so as to have almost any kind of property desired.

6 However, plastics usually are derived from the molecules in oil and gas, and oil and gas aren't going to last forever. When oil is gone, plastics, for the most part, will be gone as well. Then, too, plastics are inflammable and liberate poisonous gases when burned.

7 Well, then, are there any other alternatives? How about getting back to basics, to the rocks that human beings used before they developed the sophisticated way of life called civilization. Rock remains far more common and cheaper than either metal or plastics. Unlike plastics, rock doesn't burn; and unlike metal, rock doesn't rust. Unfortunately, rock remains just as brittle now as it was during the Stone Age. What can be done about that?

8 It might be possible to treat rock so that it loses some of its brittleness. That will, of course, make it more expensive, but it would be infinitely more useful, and, as in

the case of metals long ago, the usefulness might more than make up for the expense. This is all the more possible as the expense becomes more minimized.

9   For instance, different rocks can be combined and treated in such a way as to make the powdery substance called Portland cement. Water is added, and molecules of water *adhere to* the molecules in the powder, causing that powder to set into the hard, rocklike cement. As the cement dries, however, some of the water evaporates, leaving tiny holes behind. It is the presence of these holes that makes the cement brittle.

10 Scientists who work with cement have been developing ways of treating it during preparation in such a way as to make the holes formed by water evaporation much smaller than they would be ordinarily. The brittleness disappears, and the result is cement that can be bent, that is springy, and that won't shatter on *impact*.

11 It is important to search for a way of forming this tough cement that would involve as little labor and energy as possible. Scientists who work with materials are trying to find ways, for instance, of *converting* rocks into glassy materials without using the high temperatures required to form glass in the old-fashioned way. They also are trying to form ceramics and refractories (rocky materials that can be heated to very high temperatures and then cooled again without being changed in the process) in ways that consume little energy.

12 If all this works out, the result may be relatively cheap stone that has all its own excellent properties plus some of those associated with metals and plastics. These developments could bring about a high-tech stone age that will mean a civilization far less wasteful of energy, far less concerned with preventing fire and rust, and far less subject to the disaster of dwindling resources.

brittle—breaks easily
chipped—hacked away small pieces in order to shape it
shatter—break into many small pieces
blunted—lost its sharp edge
adhere to—stick to
impact—a blow
converting—changing to something else

Post-Reading Activities

A. The characteristics of the following materials are described: rock, metal (iron and steel), aluminum, plastics, and high-tech rock. Fill in the table on page 72 with the positive and negative features of each type of material:

Type of Material	Positive Features	Negative Features
Ancient rock	long-lasting	brittle
iron		
steel		
aluminum		
plastics		
high-tech rock		

B. Two important ways of evaluating materials are discussed—usefulness and expense.

The usefulness of materials is evaluated mostly by the ease with which they can be molded into shape and by their resistance to deterioration over time. If materials are: (a) available in abundance and are easily extracted from their sources, and (b) do not require special treatment, then they are low in expense.

Fill in the following table, evaluating the features of each material on a scale from 1 to 3. 1 = considerable (a lot), 2 = only to some extent, 3 = very limited.

	Old Rock	Metal (iron–steel)	Alumi-num	Plastics	High-tech rock
usefulness molding into shape	3	1	1	1	1
resistance to deterio-ration					
expense resources					
extraction					
treatment					

Turtle May Be Clue to Dinosaur Demise

Pre-Reading Tactics

A. Look at the **title:**
Written in newspaper headline style, the title contains the main idea of the selection. Make sure you understand *demise*. Notice, too, how many of the **key expressions** have a meaning related to the main idea.

B. Vocabulary awareness—Learn the meaning of these **key expressions:**
vanished—disappeared
the fate of (dinosaurs)—the destiny
extinction—referring to something that existed but does not exist anymore
succumb (to)—give in to
   Fill in the above **key expressions** in the following sentences:
   Many animals and plants that existed thousands of years ago _____ from the face of the earth. We don't know exactly what their _____ was and what happened. The _____ of ancient animals is of interest to some scientists who are trying to study the past. Their findings may also be important for the future, so that we know what things we should not _____ to if we want to maintain our world of today.

C. Understand the **organization** of the article by watching for paragraphs that:
   1. give background information about dinosaurs;
   2. explain why it is important to understand the demise of dinosaurs;
   3. tell what turtles might have to do with dinosaurs;
   4. present various hypotheses, not facts, about what might have happened to dinosaurs.

D. Read the selection without using your dictionary. You can do it!

Turtle May Be Clue to Dinosaur Demise

by Betty Ann Kevles

1 The turtle and the dinosaur—the first *diminutive* in size, sea-dwelling and four-legged, the second gigantic, land-roving and bipedal—seem as remote from each other in function as they are in form. Yet research into the ways of turtles may explain the greatest mystery of the dinosaurs.

2 After *dominating* this planet for about 150 million years, the dinosaurs vanished. Some evolutionary biologists see a genetic shadow of their presence in modern-day lizards. Others suspect that warm-blooded, feathered dinosaurs were the ancestors of living birds. But neither iguana nor pelican resembles the dinosaur's great size.

3 Unique to its era, the fate of the dinosaurs has *perplexed* scientists for more than a century. So complete was their disappearance that humanity was unaware of their existence until the 19th Century.

4 Although their bones had been lying beneath the soil, quite literally for ages, no one had ever *unearthed* one before. As North America was settled, dinosaur *fossils* turned up in New England, Virginia, New York, and finally in Wyoming, Utah and Montana. The great age of paleontology happily overlapped with the westward movement. A few fossils were also found in Britain and the Gobi Desert, but none in as great quantities as the American West.

Biblical Animals

5 The first people to dig up the fossils could not possibly recognize what they were. But their great size did give pause. Through an *idiosyncratic interpretation* of scripture, some theologians advanced the belief that biblical animals had been monumental and they hailed these giant bones as the remnants of Noah's animal passengers. (According to this theory, it was only the second time around, after the flood, that God shrank the animal world to its present proportions.)

6 *Paleontology* advanced swiftly and soon the extinct animals were named dinosaurs, "terrible lizards," and classified as reptiles, ancestors of living snakes and turtles. The era in which they lived was *dubbed* the Mesozoic.

7 With the acceptance of the concept of evolution, paleontologists began disputing the nature of these creatures. Were they simply enormous reptiles? Or were they, in fact, the ancestors of modern birds? Determining whether they were reptile or proto-bird might have a lot to do with solving the greater mystery: whatever happened to them?

8 In an age when our own species, Homo sapiens, ponders survival, it seems particularly important to find out what happened to the reptiles that dominated this planet for so long. Did they succumb to a single catastrophe? If so, what? Or did they survive by evolving into one or more of the species alive today?

9 Extinction, the dying out of a species, can result from a variety of causes. An enemy as small as a bacterium could have been the villain. Like the recently vanished human inhabitants of Tasmania, the dinosaurs could have been downed by disease. Or like the primate inhabitants of the disappearing rain forests, they could

have been felled by clever hunters. Or they could have been done in by a great calamity.

Volcano Eruptions

10 This last approach got a boost recently when Berkeley physicist Louis Alvarez suggested that the Earth suffered the impact of a huge asteroid that filled the skies with *debris*. Indeed, he has claimed to find proof of this theory in layers of rock near the town of Gubbio, Italy, where ancient layers of a rare metal, iridium, suggests a galactic origin.

11 A variation on this theme places the *cataclysm* at the same time but from within the bowels of the Earth. The eruptions of volcanoes many times the size of Mount St. Helens would also have covered the earth with enough dust to lower the temperature by about 5 degrees centigrade for at least a year.

12 Which brings us to the turtles. We know that the dinosaurs, like turtles, laid eggs in the sand because nests filled with broken shells and the fossilized remains of baby dinosaurs have been unearthed in Montana. If they were reptiles like turtles, they also may have been heteromorphs,

that is to say, their sex was not determined at conception genetically by the inclusion of an x or y chromosome, as it is in birds and mammals, but rather developed while they were being incubated.

13 Zoologists at the State University of New York in Buffalo have observed how sea turtles develop into males or females. Turtle eggs that lie in the sand at cool temperatures produce male turtles. And eggs that incubate at about 5 degrees higher produce females. Likewise, eggs hatched in plastic boxes at cool temperatures produced boy turtles, and warmer boxes netted girls.

14 If dinosaurs were like modern turtles, a sudden drop in temperature for even a short time may have simply eliminated all females from the species. Under stress, some female lizards that are alive today, reproduce hermaphroditically, that is, all by themselves. But male lizards cannot manage on their own.

15 The world of the dinosaurs may have ended initially with a bang, as volcanoes erupted or an asteroid crashed. But then, as lonely males sought fruitlessly for mates, it may have simply faded away, with a whimper.

demise—to die out

diminutive—very small

dominating—being the controlling species

perplexed—puzzled

unearthed—discovered

fossil—the remains of an animal

idiosyncractic interpretation—a highly personalized viewpoint

paleontology—the science of the forms of life in former geological periods

dubbed—called

debris—fallout in the sky from the impact of an asteroid hitting the earth

cataclysm—a tremendous upheaval caused by natural forces such as a volcano erupting

The real reason dinosaurs became extinct

Post-Reading Activities

A. Find the **function** of each paragraph:

Write in the number of the paragraphs(s) (one or more) which fit the descriptions below:

1. _____ Relates the demise of dinosaurs to the question of Homo sapiens' survival.

2. _____ Relates modern turtles with dinosaurs because both are known to lay eggs in the sand.

3. _____ Presents an interpretation of what might have happened to dinosaurs, utilizing both the cataclysmic event hypothesis and recent findings about turtles.

4. _____ Presents theories about natural cataclysms that might have brought a great calamity to the earth in the Mesozoic period.

5. _____ Gives a history of modern scientific activity in looking for the remains of dinosaurs.

6. _____ Outlines an early hypothesis about dinosaurs which interpreted their existence in relation to Biblical stories.

7. _____ Reports that paleontologists do not agree about the nature of dinosaurs.

8. _____ Gives a summary of the reproductive process of modern sea turtles.

9. _____ Gives examples of species that have become extinct for a variety of reasons.

10. _____ Catches the reader's attention by implying that a very small animal might be able to shed some light on the extinction of a very large one.

B. Read **between the lines:**

The writer focuses on one scientific hypothesis. But as you found out in A (above), the argument is not presented in a straightforward order. Instead, the writer leaves it to the reader to link ideas together. At the same time there is one crucial link in the chain of ideas which the reader must infer from the text—or read between the lines.

Read the statements below (1–6) which trace the writer's argument. Select sentence a, b, or c to fill in the missing idea in No. 5.

    a. The connection with turtles proves that dinosaurs were vegetarians.

    b. The dust and debris from a cataclysm blocked the sun's warmth, thus lowering the earth's temperature for at least a year.

    c. Both dinosaurs and modern turtles lay eggs; therefore, the reproductive system of dinosaurs was the same as that of modern turtles.

1. Various hypotheses have been made suggesting that catastrophic natural events destroyed the dinosaurs.

2. Dinosaurs were reptiles that laid their eggs in the sand.

3. If they were like modern turtles that also lay their eggs in the sand to reproduce, the sex of dinosaurs may have been determined by the temperature of the sand. The process could have been interrupted by a natural catastrophe that affected the earth's temperature.

4. It has been theorized that a volcano errupted or an asteroid struck the earth in the Mesozoic period, producing great quantities of dust and debris.

5. _____

_____

_____

6. Dinosaurs died out because eggs containing females did not hatch.

Third Selection
4,000-Year Search for a Perfect Calendar

Pre-Reading Tactics

A. Read the **title** to understand the main theme of the article.
Do you think the article will:
1. Describe a perfect calendar that is attainable.
2. Describe man's search for a perfect calendar?
3. Describe how throughout history people have adapted their institutions to the conditions of the planet on which we live?

B. Vocabulary Awareness—Learn the meaning of these **key expressions:**
lunar month—measured by the moon
solar year—measured by the sun
vernal equinox—the time when the sun crosses the equator in the spring, with the result that day and night are of equal length (falls approximately on March 21st)
leap year—a year which contains an added day or an added month
centennial year—the 100th year
Look for these expressions in the following article.

C. Look for the **organization:**
This article is straightforward and easy to follow as it presents an outline of the history of calendars.

Scientific View
4,000-Year Search for a Perfect Calendar

by Isabel R. Plesset

1 For thousands of years, people all over the world have pursued the unattainable objective of creating a perfect calendar. Calendar making is not a science, but it does require an understanding of the natural phenomena that determine climate, the tides, the days and nights and seasons, to all of which living things on Earth must adapt. The calendar maker's job is to find ways of grouping days to meet the needs of human beings.

2 As we now know, the basic problem is that there are 29.53059 days in a lunar month, and 365.242199 days in the solar year. If that seems like a mess, it doesn't change anything. The orbits of the Moon and the Earth, the rotation of the Earth on its own axis, the periods of the Moon's phases and the Earth's rotation around the Sun are in no way affected by human perception of them.

3 Along the road to the acquisition of this precise knowledge, calendar makers devised various ways of *reconciling* these *irreconcilables,* but as people became accustomed to each modification over periods of centuries, they resisted each new change. This human resistance to change in well-established patterns of life constituted a second great problem for the calendar makers.

4 Beginning about 2000 BC, the Stonehenge people of England created precise measuring devices, using enormous stones, but we have little idea of how they made use of their astronomical measurements. By that time, Chinese astronomers had a sophisticated knowledge of the number of days in a solar year, but we don't know how they made these determinations. The calendar most widely used today for agriculture, for business and trade, and for historical purposes is the Gregorian calendar, but for other purposes, there are many other calendars.

Gregorian's Origins

5 The Gregorian calendar had its origins in a practical calendar of 365 days, devised by the Egyptians. They divided the year into three seasons of four months each, called Flood time, Seed time, and Harvest time, corresponding to the annual cycle of the rise and fall of the Nile upon which their agriculture depended. They used the ris- ▶

reconciling—bringing together
irreconcilables—things seemingly not possible to reconcile

ing of the morning star, Sirius, to predict the annual inundation of the Nile, and from this same source they came to recognize that the solar year is not just 365 days but about 365¼ days. Their astronomers created a second calendar by which they kept track of the loss of one-fourth of a day each year, and just let the observance of their New Year slip out of phase by that amount. They knew that in 1,460 years, their civil calendar would come around again to coincide with their astronomical calendar.

6 Julius Caesar recognized that the chaotic calendar he inherited from the Roman Republic was badly out of phase with the equinox. With the advice of an Alexandrian astronomer, the Julian calendar was created and put into proper use by Augustus Caesar in the fourth year AD. It designated the first of January as the beginning of the year, and distributed the days among 12 months in a manner that made concessions to various social, political and religious practices. It introduced the device of leap year, adding one day to the month of February every fourth year.

Correcting an Error

7 The Julian calendar served Western Europe for 1,500 years, even as it became known that it contained a still further, although tiny, error. By 1545, the vernal equinox, which was used in determining the date of Easter, the most important Christian holiday, had moved 10 days from its proper date. Once again, the calendar was revised, this time resulting in the Gregorian calendar, announced in a *papal bull* in the year 1582, just 400 years ago. The error of 11 minutes 14 seconds per year was corrected by the provision that no centennial years should be leap years unless they were exactly divisible by 400. Thus 1700, 1800, and 1900 were not leap years, but the year 2000 will be. Thus also, the problem of reconciling the lunar and solar irreconcilables has been resolved in a reasonably tidy fashion, but the problem of human resistance to giving up traditional times of observances has been only partially resolved.

8 The Hebrew calendar, for example, is based on the determination of the most important Jewish holiday, the Passover. Neither the Christians nor the Jews wished to have Easter and the Passover coincide, so much of the elaborate calculating that produced the Gregorian calendar was to guarantee that such a coincidence never would occur. Now the Jews celebrate the New Year in the fall,

even though they use the Gregorian calendar for civil purposes. Similarly, millions of Chinese, Muslims in many nations, Hindus and many other people celebrate the New Year and other holidays at times dictated by their own traditions.

9 Our calendar makers may not have created a "perfect" calendar, but they appear to have set a *valuable precedent*. They have applied scientific knowledge and precision where it was appropriate to do so, and yet have maintained the flexibility required for humanistic institutions and practices. What more can we ask of anyone?

papal bull—an order issued by the Pope
valuable precedent—an action which is repeated because it makes sense

Post-Reading Activities

A. Complete the empty boxes in the grid with information from the article.

Time	Cycle	Type of Calendar
Ancient Egyptians	_____ _____	365 days in a solar year
Julius Caesar	Social, political, religious practices	_____ _____
_____ _____	Religious and civil needs	365 days and a leap year every four years

B. In a group, **talk about** these issues:

1. Why can't we find a perfect calendar?

2. Why are different calendars used throughout the world, yet there is a universally accepted calendar for civil purposes as well as for agriculture, business, and trade?

3. Try to find out more about the Stonehenge people. Where were they mentioned previously in this unit?

4. What is the thematic connection among the three selections in this unit?

Unit Six

Getting Along With Each Other

Background Information for Unit Six

Reading about how other people get along with each other in families gives us a chance to look at our own personal relationships from new perspectives. When a writer tells the reader how she/he feels about her/his brothers and sisters, parents, and even husband or wife, it is like having a conversation with a close friend. The writer confides in the reader, using the process of self-expression through writing to clarify her/his own ideas.

The selections in this unit deal with family and personal relationships, moving from a viewpoint on sibling rivalry to an account of communication between a daughter and her mother, and then to an examination of marriage, 1980-style. In the first two selections, the writers tell us about their own experiences, while in the article on modern couples, Ellen Goodman comments on the relationship she observes between her two friends, a woman and a man who have decided to marry after a long period of coupling. Through her newspaper column, this particular writer's opinions on modern life are read by thousands. You can also find Ellen Goodman's articles in book form.

Of Sibling Rivalry and Sibling Pride

Pre-Reading Tactics

A. Look at the **title:**

The word *sibling* is the key to understanding the title. Do you think the author is altogether certain about his feelings towards his brothers and/or sisters?

B. Understand the author's point of view:

The author describes the members of his *immediate family* (paragraph 1), his parents and brothers and sisters. However, in many parts of the world people have larger or extended families.

C. Vocabulary Awareness—Learn the meaning of these **key expressions:**

Complete the missing word in the passage below by using the following list:

rivalry
ambivalent feelings
jealous
sibling(s)
compete/competition
pride
envy

In most families brothers and sisters c _____ for things such as attention and parents' love. If this c _____ among s _____ s becomes real r _____ then life at home is not very pleasant for the competing siblings. Yet in most cases s _____ have a _____ _____: on one hand they love their brother or sister and on the other hand they feel j _____ of him/her. Sometimes later in life, when they are adults, the a _____ _____ produce both e _____ and p _____ in the success of the other s _____.

Of Sibling Rivalry and Sibling Pride

by Paul O'Brien

1   *Sibling rivalry* has been around, I imagine, since immediate families began dwelling alone, together. I consciously feel its jolt now, for the first time in my 25 years. Its power is bittersweet. In this case mostly sweet.

2   When my brother called last year, I could feel his enthusiasm over the phone. I could see him—his feet nervously shifting, his shoulders bouncing, his smile enlarged, showing the few lines in his 38-year-old face. The news: His book would be published by spring—"in hardback," he emphasized.

3   The pride sent chills through me. The hairs on my arms stood at attention. My heart pounded with his. I wanted to scream and cheer and jump and tell the world. So did he, I know, but we both sat at our desks in our employers' quiet offices, somehow restraining our emotions.

4   I've been one of his most loyal fans since he wrote the first page and read it to me over the phone. I read the rough draft and was moved. I offered minor criticisms. I read the manuscript and prayed that a publisher would be found. I read the initial correspondence from an interested editor and swelled with pride. I joyously encouraged positive thinking.

5   Today, and from this day on, I will enjoy his success, *albeit* vicariously. At the same time, I feel the awakening of some crude instinct. I try to deny it and cannot.

6   Envy. Jealousy. These are the evils that rot so much so swiftly. I recognize their *nascent* forms and try to reject them, but I know that I can no more dismiss their power than my dog can avoid cleaning his plate. I only hope that in acknowledging the corrosive emotion I can drive myself to overcome it.

7   As a published writer (of articles), I feel the rivalry perhaps more than our other siblings. We are five, all enjoying professional and intellectual pursuits of our own, each lending pride and encouragement and some ▶

sibling—a brother or a sister
rivalry—conflict arising between two people in pursuit of the same goal
albeit—although
nascent—at the beginning of existence

Of Sibling Rivalry and Sibling Pride—cont'd

reason for healthy rivalry to the others. As the youngest, I search for "the answers" partly through them and deeply within myself.

8   The most recurring thought throughout my observations of my brother's success has been: Maybe now I can finish a book (I've begun two) and experience similar success. My competitive nature surges, building toward the rivalry that may one day exist. That suggests (in my subconscious?) that the rivalry will be two-sided.

9   In this experience with my brother, I have learned something about our culture. It is not competition that ruins relationships—among nations, peoples and families—but jealousy, envy and greed.

10   I will write my books. I will encourage my brother to write more books. I will read them whether published or unpublished, well-received or ill-received. He, I know, will read mine. And, if we're lucky, our "rivalry" will never be anything but healthy, positive and fun. But until I've accomplished success in my own mind I will feel the bitter sweetness.

11   Our parents may revel in the successes of their offspring as outrageously and biasedly as they want, just as they have shown singular outrage at our failings—sins that outsiders would ignore. If they were to comment on the ambivalent feelings that I've expressed here, they'd call them silly.

12   No matter. I love my brother, and that will get me past the baser feelings. Nevertheless, until I know that I am over this spell, I will watch my dog while he eats, and wonder. I will wonder how different I am from him.

Paul O'Brien is a writer who lives in California. His brother, Gregory O'Brien, is the author of "Lenin Lives!" (Stein & Day).

Post-Reading Activities

A. Understand the relationships:

The writer gives information about the family members which helps the reader understand their relationships, or how they feel about each other. Find the information in the text.

1. What is the reader told about the brother?

    Example:

    —he works in a quiet office

    —he is 38 years old

2. What is the reader told about the writer of the article?

_____

3. What is the reader told about their parents?

_____

4. What is the reader told about other siblings in the family?

_____

B. Evaluate the writer's message:

In small groups, or with a partner, **talk about** these questions:

1. Paragraphs 2, 3

How does the writer help you know that the conversation is over the telephone? What is the quality of this telephone-talk that makes you recognize that it is between two brothers who know each other very well?

2. Paragraph 8

The writer compares his inability to put down (nascent) forms of envy and jealousy . . . any more than ''my dog can avoid cleaning his plate.'' Why does he compare his own behavior with a dog's?

3. Paragraphs 8, 10

How does the writer hope to use the experience of his brother's success to influence his own life?

4. Paragraph 9

How does he relate his feelings about his brother's success to the broader world in which he lives?

5. Paragraph 12

In the last paragraph, the writer again introduces a comparison of himself with his dog as he watches the animal eat. In the end, is the writer really free of sibling rivalry?

C. Talk about your own family with a partner.

Tell your partner about your own family: who are your brothers and sisters? what are your relationships with them? what are your relationships with your parents?

Words Fail Her in Chinese Language

Pre-Reading Tactics

A. Look at the **title:**

The title describes what happened to the writer or "her." But the selection itself is written from the writer's point of view; the writer tells about her own experiences with the Chinese language. From the title only, do you think that more than words alone failed her? What else failed her? What can "words failed her" also imply?

B. Listen to the **writer's voice:**

1. The writer expresses personal thoughts about her Chinese background. She uses prose, but she also includes two brief narrative (story) sections to illustrate the main idea. As you read, look for these two narrative sections.

2. As you read, you may find that the writer is talking to you, directly and personally. If you feel this way, the writer has succeeded in communicating her message.

C. Vocabulary Awareness—Learn the meaning of these **key expressions:** Match expressions in A with words in B.

A	B
1. feels frustration	_____ does not belong/is away from her natural environment
2. words fail her	_____ cannot express herself in a verbal form
3. she has difficulty with communication	_____ cannot do what she wants to do
4. she feels uprooted	_____ cannot make her ideas come across

Words Fail Her in Chinese Language

by Mabel Wong Hogle

1   Quite probably, no one appreciates the power and magic of the written word more than a writer and a teacher. Since I am both, my inability to write with any power and magic to my mother is one of the most enduring frustrations of my life.

2   My mother is the only person to whom I write in Chinese. She was born and reared in China, and it is only because of her that her four American-born children know any Chinese at all. Although we can converse in her language, our fluency is elementary. Our literacy is less than that.

3   Asian immigrants have flooded the United States in recent years, and much has been written about the immigrants' need and efforts to learn English and their problems in adapting to the American culture. But my situation is the reverse, and no less trying. I am an American attempting to reach back to an ancestral language in order to communicate with an immigrant, non-English-speaking parent. And I constantly find myself at a loss for words, *groping* in a dark, empty *chasm* for words I do not know or only dimly recollect. There are Chinese words that will speak what I mean—words that will free me of my silence. I grasp at anything to dig them out; but they were never planted in my mind, and I unearth nothing. This happens whenever I speak to my mother in ordinary conversation.

Writing, of course, is just as difficult, if not more.

Special Schooling

4   Unlike many other Chinese of my generation born in the United States, I was not formally schooled in the Chinese language as a child. My parents enrolled my older brother and sister in a Chinese school for six years, where they studied Chinese speech, reading and writing two hours everyday after attending regular American public grammar school. Since the two oldest children never used and consequently never retained what they learned, my mother decided against the expense of such schooling for her two younger daughters. Both of us later studied Chinese in college.

5   Written messages are not necessary since I see my mother frequently, but the writer in me insists I communicate to her through the written form of her language. I can never write her a poem or an eloquent *piece of prose*. Throughout my school years, whenever I wrote a paper of which I was particularly proud, I felt *chagrined* that my mother could never read it. Those were times when it made me sad to know that my mother, a product of a different, faraway world, did not even think, let alone read or write, in the same language as I. Nevertheless, I do write to her, even if it is only short notes to accompany my ▶

---

groping—searching with uncertainty (to grope in the dark)

chasm—a deep hole without a bottom

piece of prose—writing which is neither fiction nor poetry

chagrined—disappointed and embarrassed

gifts to her or post cards whenever I am out of town.

6   There is pleasure in writing Chinese characters, but for me, the writing is also woefully slow and tedious. I must look up almost every character in my English-Chinese dictionary. A stroke or a dot deleted or misplaced or misdirected would change the entire word. And to my mother, such an error is inexcusable. I know only a handful of Chinese characters by heart—among them the three words *I love you*.

Broth for Christmas

7   One Christmas, I gave my mother, among other things, 24 cans of Swanson clear broth because my supermarket had a sale on them, and because my mother uses the broth almost every time she cooks a Chinese dish. Being Chinese is equivalent to being *frugal* and practical, so I thought this would be a perfect gift. I placed one can of broth, surrounded by white tissue paper, in a box and wrapped the box prettily. On the can was taped a note explaining that she was to get 23 more cans of broth. First, I had to look up such words as *give, 23, cans, chicken, soup* and *Merry Christmas*.

8   Then I had to practice writing the characters to make sure I wrote them correctly and as beautifully as I could make them, for Chinese writing is not only a means of communication but also an art form. The note amounted to three short sentences, but it took me more than an hour to complete it. On Christmas Eve, when she opened the gift, she was *baffled* by the one *mundane* can of chicken broth. But then she saw the note and read it with much amusement.

9   When I go away on trips, I welcome the opportunity to write to my mother because, being on vacation, I can take time and unhurried effort to write. I pack my English-Chinese dictionary in my suitcase and reserve an hour or so every few nights to pen her a description of my whereabouts and happenings. She delights in my feeble, elementary attempts to write to her in her native language.

10   There was a time when I did write Chinese nearly every day. Three years of studying the language at USC was followed by a letter-writing period of my life when I studied and traveled to Europe for six months. It was the first time I was ever away from home, and I was homesick and lonely. I wrote many letters—28 to my mother, some of them five-to-six pages long. There was so much I wanted to express to my mother in those letters—not only my love, but also my understanding.

Hoped to Return to China

11   I wanted her to know that I appreciated then even more the emotional wrench it must have been for her to *uproot* herself from her homeland, family and friends to follow her husband overseas to begin an entirely different life in a foreign land. In addition, she had to suffer the tragedy and hardship of being widowed young, with four children to bring up. She had always yearned and hoped to return to China; consequently, she never made the effort to learn English.

12   Somehow, in my correspondence, I succeeded in communicating these feelings to her, for she told me that my letters touched her, many of them making her cry. And many letters made her laugh, too. I was pleased to have been able to communicate,

but I knew that my young adult thoughts and feelings were being expressed in unsophisticated, fifth-grade Chinese words and sentences.

13　My Chinese writing must be in many ways like the English writing of Asian foreign-born students, many of whom I have had in my English classes in the public high school where I teach. Such a student's English composition is immediately recognizable because of his handwriting, *contorted* syntax and awkward, inappropriate use of English idioms. I make some allowances for this student's grammatical errors and evaluate his paper keeping his language difficulty in mind.

14　I often forget that my mother makes allowances for my writing as I do for the writings of my foreign-born students. She sees my errors, tells me about them, but praises me for my labors. She is aware that I write in Chinese to please and honor her.

15　I am ever frustrated by the language barrier between us, ever yearning to phrase my thoughts to her with grace as well as precision. Unfortunately though, eloquence in writing is a gift I can never give her. But even though she can never read firsthand what I write in English, she knows the paramount meaning I want to communicate—the feelings I have for her, which have come across not through polished Chinese writings, but more definitely through the time-consuming and painstaking effort I have put into those writings. I should take heart then in knowing that I have indeed succeeded in communicating to her through the written word, however imperfectly.

Hogle is a teacher.

frugal—thrifty
baffled—puzzled
mundane—everyday style; not fancy
uproot—to pull up one's roots
contorted—not in normal order

Post-Reading Activities

A. Retaining new vocabulary:

In Paragraph 4, the writer tells us that "the two oldest children never used and consequently never retained what they learned" (in the Chinese language). This activity gives you an opportunity to use and try to retain new vocabulary and key expressions that you have already read in this unit.

Talk over your answers to the questions below with a partner.

B. Select *five* questions to answer by **writing** a few sentences for each in which you make use of the key expression.

　1. What is your main *frustration* in life? Do you think it will be an enduring frustration?

2. Have you ever had your *words or thoughts* fail you? What happened? What did you do?

3. The writer's mother *uprooted* herself in order to follow her husband overseas. Has anyone in your family had a similar experience?

4. The writer characterized Chinese people as being *frugal* and practical. Do you consider yourself frugal and practical? Why or why not?

5. Did you ever search your memory but were unable to *unearth* anything? What happened? Did you feel frustrated?

6. It is an *emotional wrench* to leave one's husband, family, and friends. In the last year have you experienced anything that gave you an emotional wrench? It might have been from reading a book or watching a film.

7. Communicating one's ideas and feelings in a new language can be quite difficult. Describe one incident when you had trouble making your feelings *come across* in English.

8. The writer tells us that she *groped in a chasm* for words, or she groped in the dark for the words with which to express her thoughts. Have you had this experience? Tell about one incident.

9. Do you think the *relationship* between the writer and her mother was close? Can language interfere with people's personal relationships? Have you ever had an experience in which this occurred?

10. The writer describes her students' *awkward* and *inappropriate* use of idioms in English. Have you ever heard someone using idioms in your native language awkwardly and inappropriately? Tell about one such incident. What did you say or do?

C. In the article the writer gives two examples of individuals talking to someone who is learning a new language.
In your own words, tell what happened:

1. **Paragraph 12**

   The mother's response to her daughter's letters written in Chinese.

2. **Paragraph 13**

   The writer's response to her students' compositions written in English.

Couples in Crisis: Negotiating Their Way to Happy Marriages

Pre-Reading Tactics

A. Look at the **title** and the **by-line:**
  1. Try to predict if the article is about:
     a. traditional marriage
     b. liberated marriage
     c. a new kind of marriage
  2. Ellen Goodman often writes about women in today's world, usually expressing ideas that describe the direction in which people are moving before they realize it themselves. She writes with a distinctive style, making each word count. Sometimes she deliberately uses words and phrases that can be understood in more than one way.

B. Follow the **organization:**
  The article has three parts; look for them as you read.

  Paragraphs 1–6
  —give an example of a negotiated marriage between the writer's two friends.

  Paragraphs 7–12
  —give the writer's general comments on marriage.
  Paragraph 13
  —gives a summary statement in which the writer's two friends are brought in again.

C. Vocabulary Awareness—Learn the meaning of these **key expressions:**
  Choose the most suitable word or expression to complete the sentences.
  1. In order to reach some agreement they need to _____ their differences.
     a. trade
     b. negotiate
     c. liberate

2. A marriage that allows the husband and wife a lot of freedom is a
_____ marriage.
   a. liberated
   b. good
   c. complicated
3. After discussing their differences for many hours the partners finally
agreed on a _____.
   a. struggle
   b. conflict
   c. compromise
4. After the divorce the children stayed with their mother, by mutual
_____.
   a. consent
   b. difference
   c. discussion
5. They felt better after they _____ _____ their differences.
   a. hammered out
   b. opened up
   c. took up

A traditional wedding in the United States

Couples in Crisis: Negotiating Their Way to Happy Marriages

by Ellen Goodman

1   I have two friends who have just passed the couples crisis, a kind of midterm exam for commitment in the 1980s. The crisis began, as it often does, when each part of this unmarried pair was offered an ideal job in another city.

2   These long-distance callings forced them to evaluate what they had assumed for the past year: their desire to be with each other. Neither could be absolutely sure that his/her own bond was strong enough to resist the *centrifugal force* of their work lives.

3   In the course of this crisis two "I"'s were put onto the table, balanced against one "we": two jobs against one relationship. The tangible rewards of professional advancement— money, status—against the intangible rewards of a personal connection.

4   The crisis was even harder because my friends are still in their 20s, still young in an era when work comes first chronologically, and often emotionally. Nevertheless, these two concocted an elaborate plan of action including many basics in two-career coupledom—a one-sided move, followed by a time of commuting, then reunion.

5   When the crisis had passed I was not surprised to hear that they had decided to get married. After all, they had already done the hard part. They had hammered out a compromise. Instead of demanding a sacrifice of each other they had worked their way to a place of mutual consent.

6   The details were less important finally than the process. These friends—lawyers in love, with due apologies to Jackson Browne—completed their *prep course* for marriage in an era when the "institution" is really an open-ended negotiation.

7   I don't know quite how to *chronicle* this new pattern of negotiation. Not that long ago, in the peak days of traditional marriage, the family unit spoke with one dominant voice or one veto. Decisions about careers and geography were largely a game of follow the leader. In everyday life household chores were also divided by *hormones*. Nearly every piece of work, from kitchen duty to car repair, was pre-labeled *his* or *hers*.

8   But in marriages between equals where tasks are acquired instead of inherited, everything is *up for grabs*. Two people with two jobs, two schedules and two egos place a much greater strain on the day-to-day skills of communication and compromise.

9   I suppose that this is why the early ▶

---

centrifugal force—motion from the center outward; implication: would distance pull them apart?

prep course—preparation

chronicle—to tell the story of

hormones—substances secreted by the body; men and women secrete different hormones

up for grabs—to be negotiated

Couples in Crisis: Negotiating Their Way to Happy Marriages—cont'd

pioneers of "liberated marriages" tried to reorganize their lives with household contracts. They wanted to protect themselves against backsliding, but also against uncertainty. The contracts sometimes read like transcripts of legal proceedings for joint custody of washers and dryers. Roles were set according to days, weeks and months instead of by sex, but they were set.

10 Now it seems that what keeps marriages between equals together aren't rigid formulas of fairness, but tolerance for change, flexibility, much give-and-take and negotiating.

11 When roles are no longer separate, they overlap and open up gaps in the everyday life of couples. When there is no single permanently assigned Milk Buyer, a family refrigerator can hold two bottles or none. On any given day both, either or neither spouse may be in charge of the children's schedule or the laundry stubs or the social calendar. Over time, regular chores such as bill-keeping or gardening may belong to husband or wife, but the only permanent system that evolves is one for trade-offs.

12 This kind of marriage geometrically increases the amount of decision-making. He does not buy the car and she the rug; they do. She doesn't worry about the school system and he about the mortgage rate; they do. It triples the chances for a bad marriage to flounder on power struggles, misunderstanding and mutual withholding. It also enhances the chance of a good marriage to thrive on connection, the sense of joint venture, mutual gratitude.

13 I don't know what will happen to my lawyer friends now—a pair who settled the trial of their pre-marriage so professionally, so personally. Surely they were lucky to find a solution to this contemporary crisis, and luck is a good sign for any couple. But their eagerness to negotiate, their willingness to work it out is even more promising. It is a proper way to begin a working marriage in every sense of those words.

Ellen Goodman is a syndicated columnist.

Negotiation in marriage

Post-Reading Activities

A. Discover the stated and implied ideas:

The article contrasts three types of marriages and gives details of each. However, since the writer is stating the case for negotiated marriage, most of the article is devoted to it. Use your own background knowledge along with the writer's comments to complete a sketch of each type of marriage. Use the table for making notes that you will use during the discussion period in B (below).

Types of marriage	Roles are:	Household tasks are:	Decision-making is:
Traditional			
Liberated			
Negotiated			

B. Discuss the ideas:

In a small group, each person advocates one of the three types of marriage and argues in favor of it. Make sure each person has an opportunity to speak in favor of each type of marriage.

C. Write about your own opinions:

Do you agree with Ellen Goodman's arguments in favor of negotiation in marriage? Write a letter to the editor in which you comment on her article and also offer your own ideas about types of marriage. Look back at Selection three in Unit I to see a model for a letter to the editor.

Getting Along in the Social World

Background Information for Unit Seven

Conventions of behavior in a society, or so-called rules of politeness, are usually the result of people interacting with each other in regular and predictable ways. The major objective of such rules of behavior is to enable us all to treat each other with civility and consideration. Once such rules become acceptable, they are passed on from one generation to the next. They are perceived as cultural norms, or the "right" way to act in a social group.

Rules of behavior often reflect the thoughts and attitudes of a leading social group. But as society changes, they may no longer be suited to the new context. As a result, there are some people who are prepared to fight for the introduction of changes in our rules of behavior to suit a new societal context, while others are equally concerned to keep the old rules, mostly because they resist any kind of change.

Although each addresses a different issue, the five selections presented in this unit share a common theme relating to the conflict which arises from changes in what seem to be acceptable norms in a society. In each case, the writer presents a personal view towards such changes, inviting us as readers to agree or disagree.

First Selection

Holding On to One's Identity With a Name

Pre-Reading Tactics

A. Read the **title**:

Who do you think needs to hold onto one's identity in modern society?
Suggest several possibilities.

B. Which view does the writer take—in favor of or against holding on to one's name?

C. Vocabulary Awareness—Learn the meaning of these **key expressions:**
Note the following two expressions which are very important for understanding this selection:

  personal identity—being onself
  be adaptable—adjust easily to new or different conditions

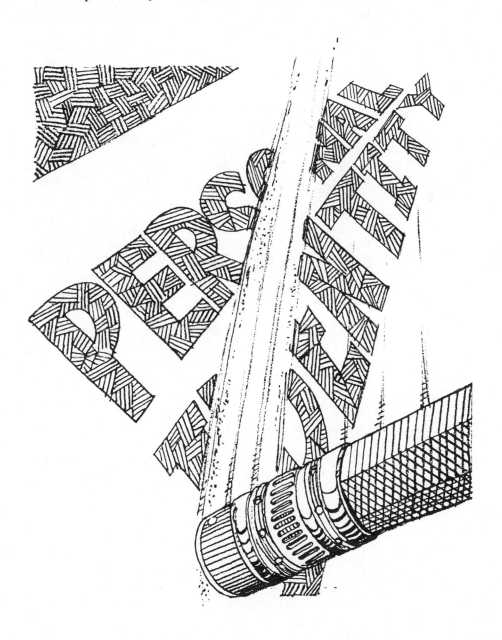

Holding On to One's Identity With a Name

by Debra Hotaling

1 "I'd never go for that," remarked a co-worker when he learned that I was keeping my own name after I got married.

2 "Why?" I asked.

3 "It's just not right—both people have to give up something for the marriage to work," he said.

4 "What would you give up?"

5 My co-worker thought about this for a moment, and then he smiled. "Other women," he said.

6 While this may be one man's failure to *leap* toward the '80s, I was surprised to learn that many people are still suspicious of a woman who keeps her birth name after marriage. It seems anti-social. (How do we address Christmas cards?) It seems *rebellious*. (She's proving a point at her husband's expense.) It seems unloving.

7 Everyone was having such fun dressing me up in my husband's name that I hesitated to interrupt them. Each time someone called me by Nick's name I had to decide: Do I bring it up or do I *let it slide?* Is it worth a fight? I felt guilty either way. Would Gloria Steinem hesitate? Would Laura Ingalls do this to Ma and Pa?

8 I discovered that some businesses do not feel *obliged* to use a woman's birth name when her husband has a perfectly good name that the woman can use. As soon as I arrived for my premarital blood test, the receptionist began erasing my last name from the file.

9 "We only file under one name," she explained. "But I'm keeping my name," I said. The receptionist looked at me and sighed. "You are getting married, right?" I nodded. "Well then," she concluded. It took several minutes of negotiations to get my last name back.

10 Even cooperative businesses seem uncertain how they should distinguish a married couple with different last names. Although our bank allowed for two names on an account, the loan officer had to attach a note of explanation on each page of our submitted loan request. She was afraid that others would think that my husband and I were "just living together." (An *unprofitable risk,* according to my bank and my mother.)

11 It got easier. After the wedding, some people continued to call me Hotaling, and some preferred to call me Vassilakis. I have learned to be adaptable and to be patient. My favorite matron aunt gently explained that my decision might be "a phase—just like when she was 5 and she wouldn't eat corn."

12 People who disagree with my decision enjoy quoting "What's in a name? . . . A rose by any other name. . . ." It's hard to argue with Shakespeare. But he was a man, and to my knowledge, he did not sign any of his works William Hathaway.

13 Like Lucy Stone, I believe that "My name is my identity and must not be lost." Stone made that statement in 1855. This is not a phase.

leap—jump

rebellious—not accepting standard, conventional ways; willing to fight for new ideas

let it slide—do not attend to it

obliged—having the obligation to do something

unprofitable risk—a situation in which the loan company, such as a bank, feels that the person getting the loan is not a safe risk

Post-Reading Activities

A. Understanding the ideas:

1. Was the co-worker mentioned in the story a man or a woman?

_____

2. In what paragraph did you find reference to the co-worker's gender?

_____

3. What was the clue which helped you?

_____

4. How did the author react to people who were addressing her by her husband's name? _____

_____

5. Why do you think businesses or other organizations have difficulty working with two different names for a married couple? _____

_____

6. What is her new husband's family name?

_____

B. In a group, **discuss** the following topic:

The writer of the article describes the custom for married women to take their husband's name which is practiced in the United States. What other countries have the same custom?

C. Take a poll:

Ask five women and five men the following question. (Try to ask people of different ages and different backgrounds.)

Do you believe women should keep their own names when they marry? Write the results of your poll in a report.

Dear Abby: Drop-in Guests Are No Strangers Abroad

Pre-Reading Tactics

A. Read the **title** of this selection. Who is ''Abby''? Where is ''abroad''?

B. People write letters to ''Dear Abby'' in order to:
(more than one might be correct)
a. get advice on a personal problem.
b. become well known to the reading public.
c. discuss important societal issues.
d. remain ''unknown'' and yet be able to disclose an intimate matter and receive an answer related to it.

C. This letter, written by Penelope, comments on one that had been written by ''Invaded.'' Abby, in turn, had also replied to ''Invaded.'' Including Abby's reply to Penelope, how many letters have been written?

　　　＿＿＿＿ 2 　＿＿＿＿ 4 　＿＿＿＿ 6

D. Vocabulary Awareness—Know the meaning of these **key expressions:**
acceptable
cultural differences
formal/informal behavior
Complete the words in the following passage:

Sometimes behavior which is a ＿＿＿＿ in one culture seems completely un＿＿＿＿ in another. Thus, in some cultures men kiss each other on both cheeks when they meet as friends, while in other cultures this kind of

behavior would look very strange. Such c＿＿＿＿ d＿＿＿＿ cause people from different cultures embarrassment if they are not familiar with these customs. Foreigners to any country in the world tend to behave in a more

f＿＿＿＿ manner since this is what they learned in school. I＿＿＿＿ behavior, when used appropriately, help the foreigner make friends in the new community.

Dear Abby:

Drop-in Guests Are No Strangers Abroad

by Abigail Van Buren

DEAR ABBY: "Invaded" complained: "My husband is from a foreign country where it is acceptable to visit people in their homes uninvited and unannounced, and even to stay overnight or for an entire weekend."

You replied: "I would like to know in which country (since the invention of the telephone) is it acceptable to drop in uninvited and unannounced for the weekend?"

Abby, your ethnocentrism is showing! In most of the world it is acceptable for family and friends to visit unannounced. My husband is from India, where visitors can arrive anytime.

Friends from northern England practice this custom, too. In fact, calling ahead is considered very formal, and a deliberate act to remove one's self from the intimate family circle.

My husband's family lives in New Delhi, India, where telephones are a luxury and not easily acquired. Last year my in-laws got a telephone after waiting for over 10 years. (The average wait is from 10 to 15 years.)

The difference in attitudes concerning drop-in visitors is a common conflict between Americans and foreigners. The explanation lies more in the cultural differences than in the personal.

PENELOPE C. SONDHI,
LINCOLN, NEB.

DEAR PENELOPE: Sorry I exposed my "ethnocentrism" (the attitude that one's own culture is superior), but since it evoked your illuminating and informative letter, it was worth it.

Post-Reading Activities

A. Discuss these questions with a partner or in a small group:

1. What various customs for visiting friends and family do you follow?
2. How might some of these customs be related to the physical conditions in the environment (availability of telephones, cars, distances, etc.)?

B. Write a "Dear Abby" letter to a friend in the group and ask him or her to answer your letter as Abby would.

Third Selection
On Rudeness and Politeness

Pre-Reading Tactics

A. Read the **title** of this selection, then look at its format:
What do you expect to find in this selection about rudeness and politeness?

B. As you read, think of which "rules" of politeness truly relate to consideration for others and which are simply conventions that have become accepted over time.

On Rudeness and Politeness

by Leticia (Tish) Baldrige

Here are some of my nominations for the most common rudenesses:

—Using a comb and cleaning one's nails in public.

—Playing a transistor radio loud enough to disturb everyone around.

—Dawdling in a telephone booth while an anxious line awaits.

—Smacking one's chewing gum or blowing bubbles into someone else's face.

—Pushing against someone without saying a sincere "Excuse me."

—Littering the restroom.

—Borrowing anything, from a cheap pen to a car, without returning it promptly and in good condition.

—Hanging up the telephone receiver before saying, "I'm sorry, I dialed a wrong number."

—Putting feet up on someone's furniture.

—Talking and making noise during a lecture or a performance.

—Sneezing without using a handkerchief.

—Making fun of someone who is different or handicapped.

—Sprawling on public transportation seats so that others can't sit down.

—Never paying a check.

—Jumping into a cab that someone else has already hailed.

—Using a toothpick in public or using one's fingers to get at bits of food.

—Not saying "Thank you" after receiving a present or being someone's guest for a meal.

And here are nominations for the most common examples of good manners:

—A man, woman or child giving up a seat on a bus for someone who looks like he or she needs it.

—Giving another a compliment when it is due; even when it is not.

—Saying "Excuse me" or "Thank you" every time either expression is applicable.

—Obeying signs posted for obvious reasons—about where not to walk, where not to park and when to keep silent.

—Holding the elevator for someone rushing to make it; holding open the post box lid for someone whose arms are full of mail.

—Helping someone carry his or her bundles when there are obviously too many to handle.

—Knocking before entering when a door is closed.

—Making sure to introduce a newly arrived stranger to the group, even if one is not too sure of all the names.

—Answering invitations promptly and sending thank-you notes for every party attended.

—Standing up when someone from the outside comes into the room and stepping forward to say hello while shaking hands.

—Talking to someone at a party who seems not to be having a good time.

—Picking up and handing to a stranger something he or she has just dropped.

—Cleaning up and straightening anything in someone else's home for which one is responsible—including dishes dirtied and games used.

—Extending a helping hand to a friend in need—like to the spouse of someone who is drunk at a party, or to the newly arrived family next door, or to a friend who has just lost a job.

Being well-mannered is really a job of relating well to one's fellow man.

Post-Reading Activities

A. Write a questionnaire:

In a group, choose five statements presented in Selection Three that indicate rudeness and five that indicate politeness. Prepare a questionnaire to find out to what extent people in your neighborhood or members of your family agree with these statements.

For example: Do you agree that the following statement is an example of polite behavior? Write 1, 2, or 3; 1 = I agree completely.

2 = I agree partially.

3 = I don't agree.

Ask ten different people to answer your questionnaire.

B. Meet with your group and compare the data you collected on your questionnaires.

C. Write your own statements of the most common examples of rudeness and politeness as they relate to your own ethnic or social group.

Fourth Selection

Addressing the First-Name Custom

Pre-Reading Tactics

A. Read the **title:**

What "custom" does the title refer to?

B. People are known by their first, by their last, or by their nickname. The English language has a number of standard nicknames. The following are some men's and women's names and their appropriate standard nicknames.

First Name (male)	Nickname
William	Bill
Richard	Dick
John	Jack
Robert	Bob
First Name (female)	**Nickname**
Elizabeth	Beth, Betty, Betsy, Liz
Margaret	Meg, Maggie, Peg, Peggy

When do we address another person by using:

the last name _____?

the first name _____?

a nickname _____?

C. Scan the subtitles of this article:

Do you find any connection between them and the main ideas? In previous articles we were able to guess the theme of the article from looking at the subtitles, but here we find that the subtitles do not tell us anything before we read the whole selection. As you read the whole selection, consider if these subtitles are clear.

D. Vocabulary Awareness—Learn the meanings of these **key expressions:**

a form of address—the manner in which we address another person in spoken interaction

first-naming—calling a person by the first name

to gain someone's respect—to behave in a manner which makes the other person respect you

civility—politeness/consideration

Use the expressions in the following paragraph:

In spoken interaction, first names and nicknames are a _____ _____ _____. The custom of *not* using a title such as Mr., Mrs., Miss, etc. is _____-_____. In order to gain _____'s _____, it is important to use the form of address which that person expects. To do so is a sign of consideration for the other person, or _____.

Addressing the First-Name Custom

by Thomas H. Middleton

I don't know that there's much we can do to change the *ubiquitous* first-name custom, but a lot of us who are over 40 would like to swing the style back to earlier, more graceful forms of address. If you are in sympathy with my thesis, please feel free to clip this column, copy it and send it to anyone you think might profit from its lessons.

What *prompts* these thoughts is two phone calls I made to my dentist in the hope of making an appointment to have my teeth cleaned and examined. Both conversations went just about like this: A young woman answered the phone, "Dentists' offices, Debbie speaking." I said, "This is Mr. Middleton. I'd like to have my teeth cleaned. I'm *overdue*."

"What is your first name?"

Figuring that she probably wanted to get my file onto her computer screen without confusing me with any other Middletons, I said, "Thomas."

"Hang on, Thomas," she said, "I'm going to transfer you to the appointments desk."

Voice of Familiarity

I hung on, suffering the *strains* of the sort of music my wife refers to as "dentist-office-elevator junk"—the sound that, paradoxically, drives you nuts because it is created seemingly for the sole purpose of not irritating anyone—and thinking, with a sublimated growl, *"Nobody* calls me Thomas." The fact is that friends and many casual acquaintances call me Tom, and people who don't know me personally *used to* call me Mr. Middleton. But this voice calling me Thomas belonged to someone who doesn't even know what I look like.

Still I hung on and hung on, hearing the junk music, but no one spoke to me. Finally, I stopped hanging on and hung up. I redialed the number.

This time, in answer to "What's your first name?" I said, "Thomas," and was about to add, "but please don't call me Thomas" when she slipped past my guard with a quick, "I'll connect you with the appointments desk, Thomas."

This time, again hearing the junk sounds and waiting for no one to pick up, I started thinking that if she had called me "Mr. Middleton" instead of "Thomas," she might have remembered who was calling, and she might even have called me back to tell me that someone was ready to make my appointment. (I'm just kidding. I'm getting soft in the head, but I'm not that far gone. She wouldn't have called me. Let my teeth *rot*, along with the rest of the head. She couldn't care less.)

It Happens Almost Everywhere

The first-naming is almost always done by people young enough to be our children. Last year, I sprained my ankle in a New York City pothole, and when I hobbled to a doctor's office, the young receptionist called my turn, saying, "This way, Tom." I noted a paradox when the doctor, who was almost exactly my age, said: "That's a very serious sprain, Mr. Middleton."

This form of address is common not simply in doctors' and dentists' offices, but almost everywhere. At a local savings and loan the other day, the young woman who was dealing with me, after checking my name out on the withdrawal slip, wished me "Merry Christmas, Thomas."

Doctors' and dentists' assistants seem to be the prime *culprits*, though. Perhaps I got a glimpse of the reason for this a few months ago when, at a party, I met a young man who had recently become a chiropractor. He told me that he had been taught in school that, as a doctor, he should call his patients, no matter what their age, by their first names, but that they should address him as Dr. Gilbert. That would gain him respect, he'd been told. We involved the entire party in the discussion, and, not surprisingly, everyone over 40 expressed great displeasure at being first-named by people whose first names they didn't even know. One lady, who had been introduced as Patty, said she was particularly irked at being called "Patricia." "No one has ever called me Patricia," she said, "except my mother when she was angry about something."

That must be especially galling—to have strangers call you Patricia, or Margaret, or Elizabeth when every one who knows you calls you Pat, Patsy, Patty, Trish or Tricia; Meg, Maggie, Peg or Peggy; Liz, Lizzie, Beth, Betty or Betsy.

Most of us are timid about being thought stuffed shirts or pompous asses if we ask to be called Mr., Mrs., Miss, or Ms. Lastname instead of our first names, but the irritation is widespread, and we really should speak up.

Over the years, I've heard from many ladies who've described what they regard as a thoroughly humiliating experience. Typically, these letters say, "Last week, I saw a doctor who was about the age of my grandson. This young man, whom I had just called, 'Dr. Jones,' said, 'Adelaide, climb up here, and we'll see about that pain in your shoulder.' This, while I was dressed in one of those awful gowns they have. The whole experience is demeaning, and the 'Adelaide' from this youngster is insufferable. I felt like calling him 'Sonny' or 'Junior,' but my upbringing prevented me."

I'm delighted to report that since I wrote the foregoing, my dentist's office phoned to tell me I was due for a cleaning and that I could have an appointment the very next morning with a hygienist named Elizabeth.

Hygienist's Civility

Elizabeth proved to be a lovely young woman who greeted me with "Mr. Middleton? I'm Elizabeth, and I have a bit of a cold, so I'll wear this mask." With or without the mask, she was lovely. As she was scraping away at the plaque, she asked, "Did I tell you my name was Elizabeth?" "Ug-ug," I replied—close enough to "Uh-huh" to be understood as an affirmative. "May I call you Tom?" she asked. I said, "Ug-ug" again, and when she took her scraper out of my mouth to give me a rinse-break, I told her about this column and congratulated her on breaking the long string of automatic firstnamism I'd been writing about, and I thanked her for her civility in asking permission.

That's all I'm talking about, I guess—civility.

My teeth have never been cleaner.

---

ubiquitous—found everywhere

prompts—initiates, brings about

overdue—later than an originally set date

strains—tension and stress

rot—decay

culprit—a person guilty of something

Post-Reading Activities

A. Discuss the custom of addressing people by their first name in your own community. Is age an important factor?

B. Why does the writer of Selection IV claim that his main concern is "civility"? Do you agree with this attitude?

Fifth Selection
Don't Call Me, I'll Call You—but Not From Cloud 9

Pre-Reading Tactics

a. Read the **title:**
Are you familiar with the expression "Don't Call Me, I'll Call You"? When do people use it?

B. Read only the **first** and **last** paragraphs of this selection. It is often possible to guess the main theme of an article from reading the first and last paragraphs. What do you think the message of this article will be? **Read** the entire article and test your hypotheses.

C. You became familiar with Ellen Goodman's writing in an earlier selection in Unit Six. It prepared you for this selection. Remember, Goodman uses language playfully. Pay special attention to her use of language as you read.

D. Vocabulary Awareness—Learn the meaning of these **key expressions:**

telephone addiction—to be addicted to the telephone, just like alcoholics are addicted to alcohol and drug addicts to drugs.
to be programmed for—your behavior can be predicted as part of addiction, programming, or strong habitual patterns.
detoxification center—a center at which "patients" can be helped in getting rid of the toxins of alcohol or drugs.

Don't Call Me, I'll Call You —but Not From Cloud 9

by Ellen Goodman

1 Forgive me if I do not herald a "new era in communications." The announcement was made last week that airplanes are now being equipped with pay telephones. But this time I'll forgo the *fanfare,* pass up the *paean* to progress. The ability to reach out and touch someone 35,000 feet below doesn't warm the cockles of my *telephone-aversive heart.*

2 Like every *red-blooded American,* I too went through an Alexander Graham Bell period. There were several years during adolescence when my left ear was continually warm, when my parents had to follow the path of the black cord, like crumbs in the forest, in order to find their lost child. I spent enough time huddled in closets with a phone to have grown mushrooms on my kneecaps.

3 Now I am convinced that the American populace is divided into two groups: those who are and those who are not able to *sever the* telephone *cord.* One of the most serious, unreported, disabling, anti-social diseases in America today is that of telephone addiction.

4 A telephone addict is defined as a citizen who cannot be away from a phone for more than three hours without suffering *anxiety tremors.* The telltale signs of telephone addiction are found in the answers to these questions: (1) Can you spend an entire day without making a single call? (2) Can you unload the dishwasher or the groceries without talking on the phone? (3) Are you more likely to phone when you are alone? (4) If you were being proposed to on one line, could you ignore the call on the other line?

5 A majority of Americans have been programmed to believe that they absolutely must pick up the phone, if only to make it stop ringing. Pavlov's dog salivated; we reach. The results of this are appalling. Consider how many babies have been dropped, blouses burned, dinners ruined and *trains of thought* derailed by the telephone.

6 The same instrument has had a dismal effect on personal relationships. Every day millions of people interrupt a conversation with someone in the same room, out of a compulsion to respond to some- ▶

fanfare—fancy introduction
paean—praise
telephone-aversive heart—feeling negative towards the telephone
red-blooded American—One hundred percent American
sever the . . . cord—cut the cord (usually the umbilical cord)
anxiety tremors—anxiety reactions
train (of thought) derailed—a train going off the rail (the train of thought is interrupted)

Don't Call Me, I'll Call You
—but Not From Cloud 9—cont'd

one on another street or in another state. Every day men and women are put to the crucial test of sexual compatibility: Do you believe in practicing telephonus interruptus?

7   It must be said that the telephone *purveyors* bear a grave responsibility for the rapid growth of addiction in the United States. Most of the so-called improvements, advances, progress in technology have been directed at the hard-core user—or shall we say abuser?

8   Think for a minute of how the pushers have encouraged this habit. We now have conference calls and video-telephones. We have phones that involve no hands. We have phones that can be programmed so that they will track us down at another location. We even have portable pet phones that will follow us wherever we go, heeling on command.

9   As the pushers know, abuse is at its absolute peak among the overachievers, the high-flyers, the Type AT&Ts who must feel *indispensable,* in control at all times. It is these souls who use the telephones in the fancy hotel bathrooms. It is these people who talk into receivers at restaurant tables. It is these people who have phones put in their cars. Indeed, there are

some frequent phoners who log enough long-distance miles a week to win a trip to Singapore.

10   Until now there was one remaining telephone-free environment: the airplane. The Transcontinental 1011s, DC-10s and 727s acted as detoxification centers for people trying to take the cure. Yes, some abusers broke down 35,000 feet above Illinois, and were found sweating and reciting their credit-card numbers over and over.

11   But there were success stories, too—men and women who learned what life was like without a ringing in their ears. Men and women who communicated person-to-person with seatmates. Men and women who read and watched the clouds go by.

12   Now even this refuge has been violated. Today you can make calls from selected airplanes; tomorrow you will be able to receive calls on these airplanes. What will become of those of us who do not want our airspace violated by the side effects of this ugly addiction? The need is great, the time is now: Fellow flyers, unite in behalf of a Non-Phoners' Section!

Ellen Goodman is a syndicated columnist.

purveyors—distributors, promoters
indispensable—impossible to do without

dunno—don't know

Post-Reading Activities

A. Check up on understanding:
Did you guess the message of the article correctly from just reading the first and last paragraphs before you read the whole selection?

B. There are twelve paragraphs in this article. Find which paragraphs deal with the following main themes:

1. The definition of a "telephone addict":

Paragraph(s) _____

2. The effect the telephone has had on personal relations:

Paragraph(s) _____

3. A teenager's need for constant telephone use:

Paragraph(s) _____

4. Technological development in telephone types:

Paragraph(s) _____

5. The people who are likely to become telephone addicts:

Paragraph(s) _____

C. Find the organization:
How does Ellen Goodman build her thesis by using the main topics given in the list in part B (above)? Follow the development of her argument, or the organization of the article.

D. Discuss, in a small group, the difference between use and abuse of telephone communication in modern society.

Fitness and Health

Background Information for Unit Eight

Since everyone wants to stay fit and remain healthy, what possible questions are there for discussion? After you have finished reading and thinking about the selections in Unit Eight, you will realize that there are many ways to consider the topic.

In Selection I, a veteran Boston Marathon runner (the Marathon is a famous race) tells us that he has decided to drop out of future races because the Marathon is no longer fun; it has become a race for addicts.

If you too have wondered about the effects of running, along with other forms of exercise, you will find some answers in Selection II, a comment on research into forms of exercise such as walking, swimming, jogging, climbing stairs, etc.

Just in case you are considering a trip to New York City, Selection III, "Route for Runners," will help you follow a well-planned path through the heart of Central Park. To consider, of course, is the question: is running the best form of exercise?

No matter what exercise plan you follow, good advice says that working out does more than just make you feel good. You'll read about what else it does for you in Selection IV.

First Selection
The Boston Marathon: The Passing of an American Pastime

Pre-Reading Tactics

A. Read the **title** to find the main idea:
   1. If you follow sports, or run as a hobby, you probably know that the Marathon in Boston is a long-distance race, one of the most famous.

2. The phrase *the passing of an American pastime* is a clue that the writer of the article enjoys playing with words; he has fun with them. In the title, he uses words in the same phrase that sound similar but have different meanings. Use your dictionary if you do not understand the difference between *passing* and *pastime*.
3. From (the) *passing of* we can also guess that the writer's view is:
   a. the Marathon is getting better.
   b. the Marathon is going to change.
   c. the Marathon is not what it used to be in the past.

B. Vocabulary Awareness—Learn the **key expressions:**

grievances—grounds (reasons) for complaining
protest—express opposition to something
(to) lament—mourn/express sorrow
imperil—endanger
get hooked—become addicted to

C. Look for words that place the event **in time:**
As you read, make use of the words that signal changes in time:
   a. **Paragraph 1**
      The writer begins by telling what he plans to do *tomorrow*.
   b. **Paragraph 3**
      Next, he tells how things used to be *three years ago*.
   c. **Paragraph 8**
      He tells a story about what happened in the good, old days. *I'll never forget.* . . .
   d. **Paragraph 10**
      Then, he's back in the present. *These days.* . . .
   e. **Paragraph 12**
      Finally, he gives a suggestion for the future. *Let's.* . . .

D. This selection is an example of opinion-feature writing found in a newspaper. It's meant to be entertaining, yet it presents a strong point of view.

The Boston Marathon: Passing of an American Pastime

1 Tomorrow, for about three hours, I will take part in a protest demonstration. To dramatize my grievances, I will run 26 miles 385 yards from a rural village called Hopkinton to the towering Prudential Center in downtown Boston. I will not be carrying any signs. In fact, the only thing that will distinguish me from several thousand other people who will be traveling the same route is that I won't be wearing an official number.

2 The purpose of the demonstration will be to lament the passing of a wonderful American pastime—running, as I knew it and think it ought to be—and there could be no better occasion for staging such a protest than at America's most venerable long-distance footrace, the Boston Athletic Association Marathon.

3 As I see it, running became imperiled a few years ago, in the thick of the Me Decade and just as the *Culture of Narcissism* was reaching its zenith. Suddenly, pectorally perfect Bruce Jenner and massively mesomorphic Arnold Schwarzenegger had become pop heroes, and it became chic to worry about your waistline, sagging chin, and flaccid muscles. Then, James Fixx wrote *The Complete Book of Running,* which quickly lapped all the other self-help, guru, and diet books on the bestseller lists. Overnight, it seemed, running has zoomed from weird to respectable, even fashionable. Everyone who was anyone was trotting around in 60 dollar running shoes and flashy warm-up suits from Bloomingdale's.

4 Some *trendies,* unfortunately, really got hooked. It was not enough simply to run and be run over in Central Park. *To prove your mettle,* you had to race, and of course, this meant that eventually, you had to run the ultimate race—the marathon—and the ultimate marathon—Boston.

5 Soon, what had once been a nice little neighborhood jaunt in Beantown and environs became a veritable Jock Woodstock. As the field climbed past three, then four, then five thousand runners, the race organizers, in a desperate attempt to cope with the chaos, began imposing qualifying times. Last year, any man under 40 years of age who wished to run with an official number had to have completed a certified marathon in less than three hours. Even with that restriction, though, more than 7,800 officially qualified runners showed up. This year, with the qualifying time for men under 40 lowered to a fast-stepping 2 hours 50 minutes, about 6,000 are expected to run.

6 I failed to qualify. Oh, I suppose I could have if I had been willing to spend a couple hours each day running 15 miles or more. But I'm too busy, and running is too monotonous to devote so much time to it. I still regard it as a hobby, something I do in my spare time for fun.

7 And that's the way Boston used to be—fun. When I first ran in the marathon way back when I was a skinny high-school senior, there were only 900 runners at the starting line. I wound up dropping out after 17 miles; actually I nearly passed out and had to be carted into Boston in an ambulance. Still, I got a big charge out of it because the event was so joyous and the people were so colorful and *bizarre.*

8 I'll never forget this one guy, a burly Irishman who showed up at the

starting line with some of his drinking buddies. His hairy beer belly was only partially covered by a Beethoven sweatshirt. He was wearing plaid Bermuda shorts that nearly touched his knees, dark, over-the-calf socks and torn-up high black sneakers. He got warmed up by downing a six-pack and belching. When the gun went off, he exploded like he was running the anchor leg of a 440-yard relay. After only about 200 yards, he suddenly pulled up short, green in the face, and anointed the curb with his breakfast.

9   That's what Boston was all about, I thought then and still think now. It's a chance for hams and shams, and desk-bound Walter Mittys to realize their dreams of athletic glory. For a few bucks, some stinging blisters, some aching joints—and some guts—any plumber or professor can rub shoulders with running's great and go home bragging to family and friends that, yes, he was there, he took part in the World Series of Running, the Super Bowl of Marathoning, and what's more, finished.

10   These days, though, the officials don't see it that way. John D. (Jock) Semple, the feisty, tough-talking Scotsman who is the assistant director of the marathon, says the unofficial runners are an *execrable* lot who are ruining the marathon. ''I hate them,'' he told me. ''I'd have 'em all shot if I could get my hands on 'em.''

11   I think Semple is overloaded on ▶

Culture of Narcissism—from Greek mythology. Narcissus was a beautiful man who admired his own reflection in the water so much that he turned into a flower called the narcissus.

trendies—people who keep up with new trends or fashions

to prove your mettle—to prove your worth

bizarre—oddly strange

execrable—to be hated

The Boston Marathon—cont'd

carbohydrates. The people who are ruining Boston are all those lean, humorless, glaze-eyed, hardcore, semi-pro addicts who will instantly numb your senses with their tedious talk about shoes and training, and times, and diet, and running as psychic phenomenon and running as mystic experience, etc., etc., *ad nauseam.*

12 So I say let's do away with the qualifying times and official numbers. Let's give running back to the barstool jockeys, the once-around-the-block joggers, the armchair athletes and weekend hackers. Let's open up the marathon and make it the great American folk celebration and rite of spring that it ought to be.

ad nauseum—to a sickening extent

Post-Reading Activities

A. Write a summary of the article by using the words that signal time. Tell what the author says:

1. **Paragraph 1**

   tomorrow
   What does he plan to do?

2. **Paragraph 2**

   the purpose *will be*
   Why will he stage a protest?

3. **Paragraph 3**

   a few years ago . . . then . . . overnight
   What happened to imperil running?

4. **Paragraph 5**

   soon . . . last year . . . this year
   What else happened?

5. **Paragraph 7**

   Boston *used to be . . . way back when*
   How did the Marathon used to be run? When was that?

6. **Paragraph 9**

   (that's what Boston) *was about . . . then* and (should be) *now*
   Does he think it should stay the way it used to be? Why?

7. Paragraph 10

these days

Who is not in favor now of the way it used to be?

8. Paragraph 12

let's

In the future, how does he propose to change things?

B. Guess word meanings:

The phrases in parentheses below should help you guess the meanings of the italicized words taken from the selection.

1. Paragraph 2

a *venerable* footrace

(It's the passing of a traditional pastime)

_____

2. Paragraph 3

pectorially perfect . . . massively mesomorphic

(Athletes have well-developed muscles; Jenner and Schwarzenegger are champions.)

_____

3. Paragraph 3

sagging chin . . . flaccid muscles

(When your waistline grows, what else happens?)

_____

4. Paragraph 4

the *ultimate* race (is the Marathon).

and the *ultimate* Marathon (is Boston).

_____

5. Paragraph 5

a *jaunt* in Beantown and environs

(Remember, the context is running.)

_____

6. Paragraph 5

Beantown (Have you tasted Boston baked beans?)

_____

7. Paragraph 8
a *six-pack* (of beer) made him *belch*
(You guessed it!)

_____

8. Paragraph 9
desk-bound Walter Mittys
(They dream of athletic glory . . . Remember, you read about Walter Mitty in Unit Two.)

_____

C. Have **fun** with these words:
These are examples of the writer's playfulness with words. Which ones did you understand?

1. Paragraph 3
. . . which quickly *lapped* the other . . . books
(The context of the article is running.)

2. Paragraph 5
Jock (from jockeys . . . men who live for sports)
Woodstock (The place where a never-to-be-forgotten rock music concert took place in the 1960s.)

3. Paragraph 7
dropped out . . . passed out
(The repetition of *out* calls our attention to the sentence.)

4. Paragraph 8
. . . green in the face, he *anointed* the curb with his breakfast
(Usually kings and saints anoint.)

5. Paragraph 9
it's a chance for *hams* and *shams* . . .
(The words sound the same; *hams* are show-offs and *shams* are phonies.)

D. **Discuss** in small groups:
1. The writer says the Boston Marathon used to be fun. Do you think sports events in general should be fun?
2. Do you have more fun participating in sports or watching them?
3. What do you think of sports fans who take the game they are watching too seriously? Do you know of any examples?

Second Selection
Exercise: Moderation is Enough

Pre-Reading Tactics

A. Read the **title** to find the main idea:
Do you think that the writer of this selection is for or against exercise? The **key word** in the title is *moderation,* which means *within reasonable limits.*

B. Vocabulary Awareness—Learn the meaning of these **key expressions:**
moderation (moderate levels)
sedentary (inactive physically)
cardiovascular system
daily routine
health benefits and health risks
physical fitness
Complete the words in the following passage using the list of words given above.
People frequently ask, ''What is ph_____ f_____?'' If we are looking for a technical answer, then we need to use measures of levels of muscular strength and endurance, heart action, balance, and coordination. If we are looking for a personal answer, f_____ has to do with how we feel in the morning, how tired or fresh we are after a day's work, etc. The d_____ r_____ of most people should include some type of exercise. People who have never been active in sports and want to start exercising should start in m_____ and not overdo activities which they are not used to. Complete lack of exercise or s_____ behavior creates greater h_____ r_____ while many studies have shown that ph_____ f_____ has h_____ b_____ for most people. Exercise at a m_____ level is beneficial to the c_____ s_____.

C. As you read the selection, ask yourself the following questions:
1. Who are the people with the least cardiovascular problems?
2. How much exercise is recommended for an average person who is not a professional athlete?
3. What questions require further research?
4. Where have I already read about James Fixx?

Exercise: Moderation is Enough

by Michael Gold

1 When author and running guru James Fixx dropped dead while jogging down a quiet Vermont road recently, the irony was inescapable: If the sport that Fixx had sold to so many Americans could kill him, then maybe it isn't such a good idea for the rest of us. Not that his death has emptied the streets of joggers, but it has raised some doubts about whether any *tangible* health benefit really comes along with the sweat.

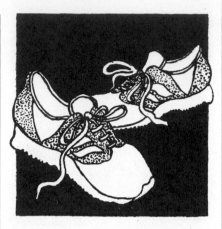

2 But just a week after Fixx's death, researchers from Harvard and Stanford universities *unveiled* a comprehensive study of roughly 17,000 men that should quiet the doubters. Not only did the 2,500 or so sedentary men in the study show significantly greater heart and circulatory disease than those who were active, they also had a death rate due to cardiovascular disease nearly twice as high as the most active group, dying on average four to five years earlier. Researchers have presumed that exercise prolongs life, but this study—because it analyzed the leisure activities of such a large group of middle-aged and older men and followed their health histories for up to 16 years—is being *hailed* as the first solid, scientific evidence for such a connection.

3 Even more significant, though, the researchers found the lower death rate and other protective benefits among men who exercised at *moderate* levels—far from the fevered pitch some people have adopted.

4 "We're not talking about an amount of exercise that's overwhelming or *overbearing*," says Ralph Paffenbarger, leader of the study and an epidemiologist at both Harvard and Stanford. "These are the kinds of things that people should be able to fit into their daily routine."

5 According to the study, the men with the fewest cardiovascular problems were those whose regular habits of walking, climbing stairs, and playing various sports caused them to burn at least 2,000 kilocalories of energy per week. Paffenbarger estimates that an hour's brisk walk will use up 450 kilocalories. "A person who does that four times a week—and maybe gets out of the elevator early to walk a few flights of stairs or does

some regular hobby work like gardening—that will get him around 2,000 or more,'' he says. ''And a person who plays an hour of racket sports three times a week would easily get into this 2,000 kilocalorie category.''

6 The men classified as least active used no more than 500 kilocalories per week in leisure-time activity. This group showed an 85 percent higher risk of death due to cardiovascular disease; their overall death rate—due to all causes—was 63 percent higher.

7 Although most previous tests have documented the health benefits of exercise only among such *hard-core* athletes as marathoners and devoted swimmers, the new Harvard-Stanford study is not completely alone in its conclusions. Scientists at the Oregon Health Sciences University recently reported that previously inactive men and women who participated in a three-day-per-week weight-training program were able to improve certain cardiovascular signs after four months. Unlike the intensive endurance activities examined in most studies, working out with weights involves only short periodic bursts of muscle movement against resistance.

8 Similarly, Peter Wood, a biochemist with the Stanford Heart Disease Prevention Program, has observed positive changes in the blood level of fatty proteins among previously sedentary men who took up jogging. Those who ran 10 miles a week—a regimen Wood calls fairly moderate— showed a 10 percent increase in high-density lipoproteins, the ones that seem to *scavenge* cholesterol. ''Of course,'' adds Wood, ''it is something of a sliding scale. The more miles you put in—within reason—the greater the reward.''

9 At the moment researchers don't know whether that sliding scale has an upper limit beyond which exercise may cause cardiovascular damage or increase the risk of sudden death among healthy people. Injuries to bones and joints, however, increase dramatically when some joggers exceed 15 miles per week.

10 As to what killed Fixx, it was heart disease that he had apparently inherited; his father died of a heart attack at age 43. According to the Vermont chief medical examiner, two of Fixx's coronary arteries were so severely blocked that he might have died that day even if he weren't running.

11 Fixx's friends and colleagues point out that he had ignored the most basic health advice to runners with family histories of heart trouble. Not only had he refused to take a stress test, he reportedly had felt warning signs—pain and ▶

tangible—realistic
unveiled—revealed to the public
hailed—announced (positively)
overbearing—too strong
hard-core—professional, fully devoted
scavenge—cleanse, or sweep out

Exercise: Moderation is Enough—cont'd

tightness in his neck—but disregarded them. For these reasons, says William Castelli, director of the landmark Framingham study of heart disease, Fixx's death says little about the general risks and benefits of exercise.

12   On the other hand, Castelli, Paffenbarger, and others say, the new evidence on the value of low-level exercise suggests it would be worthwhile for sedentary people to *get off their duffs*.

13   "It appears that an extra 1,500 kilocalories a week gets you the benefit," says Castelli. "That's roughly 15 extra miles a week—running, walking, or crawling. It's not that much."

get off their duffs—stop sitting, get up

Post-Reading Activities

A. Prepare your answers in **writing:**

1. Why is the Harvard and Stanford study considered to be comprehensive? In your answer refer to the number of people who participated in the study and the length of time which was devoted to it. Why were the earlier studies not relevant to the average member of modern society?

2. Imagine that you have a neighbor who fits the group of people who only use about 500 kilocalories per week. After reading this article, you want to give that person some advice for lowering his/her risk of death from cardiovascular disease. **Write** down the advice you are going to give your neighbor with the necessary explanations to convince him/her of the importance of moderate exercise.

B. **Discuss** in a group:

1. What are the questions relating to exercise that still remain unanswered?

2. In order to train properly for the Boston Marathon, Art Carey says that one would need to practice running 15 miles every day. How does this compare to the recommendations given in Gold's article? Do you think that there might even be some health risks involved in such a program?

Third Selection

The New York Hilton's Route for Runners

Pre-Reading Tactics

Selection III is a brochure that New York Hilton guests find in their rooms. Why do you think the Hilton management decided to make this brochure available to their customers?

THE NEW YORK HILTON'S
ROUTE FOR RUNNERS.

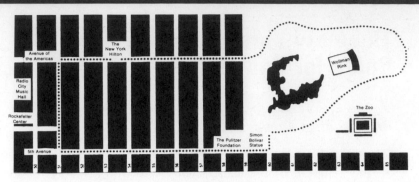

THE NEW YORK HILTON'S
ROUTE FOR RUNNERS.

We know how difficult it is to stick to a jogging routine away from home.

So, we've plotted a scenic easy-to-follow route you can take during your stay at The New York Hilton.

Start off at The New York Hilton and head uptown on Avenue of the Americas. Enter Central Park at 59th Street (the park is open for jogging daylight hours only) and take a circular route around the pond and Wollman Rink past the zoo before exiting at Fifth Avenue. Continue downtown past the Pulitzer Fountain, fashionable Fifth Avenue shops and St. Patrick's Cathedral. Take a right at Rockefeller Center up 51st Street. Then another right at Radio City Music Hall for the last stretch back to The New York Hilton.

Except for slight grades in Central Park, your 1¾ mi. (2.9 km.) run will take you along a level concrete and asphalt course.

If you'd like to lengthen your route, keep in mind that 20 uptown/downtown blocks equal a mile. And 3 crosstown blocks come to about a ½ mile.

Post-Reading Activities

A. Discuss, in a group, why the Hilton makes this jogging map available to its guests.

B. Prepare one or several jogging and walking routes for your area. Think of the number of kilocalories one could use by walking briskly along your planned routes.

Insurance: A Policy of Fitness

Pre-Reading Tactics

A. Understand the **title:**
1. The word *policy* is used in two of its meanings, resulting in a play on words:
   —a policy of fitness
   —an insurance policy
2. The article relates fitness and health to consumer information about buying life insurance. Although different types of insurance are listed, they are not important to know for understanding the link between fitness and insurance.

B. Vocabulary Awareness—Learn the meaning of these **key expressions:**
Match a word or expression in A with an expression in B.

A	B
1. criterion (sing)/criteria (pl)	_____ strenuous exercise
2. shop around	_____ become fit
3. well-being	_____ be suitable for
4. shape up	_____ look for something suitable
5. physical exertion	_____ rules or principles
6. to qualify	_____ a satisfactory condition of existence

C. Understand the **content:**
1. As you read, look for the criteria that qualify you to buy insurance at a discount.
2. As you already read in Selection Two, the research findings about the cause and effect of physical exercise and sound health may not be conclusive, but insurance companies are not waiting for the final results of research. Do you think insurance companies are taking big risks?

Insurance: A Policy of Fitness

by Peter D. Lawrence

1 Like the increasing millions of Americans who regularly follow a vigorous exercise program, I know that working out makes me *feel* good. Moreover, I am convinced it contributes to both my physical and psychological well-being. But there is an added enticement you may not be aware of: keeping healthy *may* save you insurance dollars as well. How can you trade a pound of flesh for an ounce of cash?

2 First of all, you must be a standard risk: those with dangerous professions (a stuntman, say) or hobbies (skydiving, for instance) are automatically disqualified. Beyond that, no physical exertion is actually required for the most basic health discount: the nonsmoker's life insurance discount. Because of the medical links between smoking and such major killers as heart disease and lung cancer, insurance companies have been rewarding nonsmokers with lower rates for twenty years. Today four out of five life insurance companies offer discounts averaging from 10 to 15 percent. Others—such as the Metropolitan Life Insurance Company, the country's second-largest insurer—reserve their best rate for those who meet certain health criteria. Smokers are automatically disqualified.

3 Nonsmokers' discounts are generally available for both traditional whole-life and term policies. Some companies also offer them for the increasingly popular variable and universal life policies.

4 In life insurance where the most innovative and, in some cases, the largest discounts are offered, the key is regular, strenuous exercise. At Allstate they call it Shape Up & Save. Depending on your age and the face amount of your policy, qualifying can save you an additional 15 to 30 percent beyond Allstate's normal nonsmokers' discount.

5 To qualify, you must have been a nonsmoker for at least the last twelve months and not have had your driver's license suspended or *revoked* during the last three years. For the past year, you must also have participated in one or more of the following exercises at least three times a week for at least thirty minutes on each occasion: aerobics/Jazzercise, bicycling, jogging/running, racquetball/handball; swimming, gymnastics/calisthenics, vigorous sustained walking (for at least two miles in thirty minutes).

6 In addition, you must do two out of three of the following: participate in one of the above forms of exercise at least *five* times a week for thirty minutes each time, avoid excessive salt intake, or

wear a seatbelt at least 75 percent of the time—whether driving or riding as a passenger—(or be in a vehicle equipped with an air bag). For now, Allstate's discount is available only for ten-year term policies, but it will soon be offered on its universal-life policies as well.

7 Remember, though, not to be *hypnotized* by any discount. Insurance is a very competitive business, so shop around and buy the policy that best suits your needs.

revoked—to have one's license taken away

hypnotized—put into a state in which one is susceptible to suggestion

Post-Reading Tactics

A. Understand the content:

By answering these questions in writing, you will produce a summary of the article.

1. **Paragraph 1**

Name three benefits of working out.

_____

2. **Paragraph 2**

What is a standard risk?

_____

3. **Paragraph 2**

What is the most basic health discount?

_____

4. **Paragraph 3**

What four types of insurance give a nonsmoker's discount?

_____

5. **Paragraphs 5 and 6**

To qualify for a discount on life insurance, what kind of physical exercise program must you follow?

_____

B. Discuss in small groups:

1. The topic of smokers' and nonsmokers' rights has been a controversial one in many places. Share your opinions about whose rights should be protected by law and to what extent.

2. Do insurance companies want to help you stay fit, stay healthy, or do they want to sell more insurance?

3. Should a fitness program be left to each individual's decision, or should health officials mandate programs?

C. Apply the ideas:

1. Plan a personal physical exercise program using the same criteria as insurance companies suggest.

Advancing Life Through the Search for Knowledge

Background Information for Unit Nine

In an age when business and technology dominate our attention, learning for learning's sake alone might appear out-of-style. A short-term goal such as preparing for a career is likely to be one's educational goal. A long-term objective such as seeking knowledge seems too detached from real-life concerns. But the kinds of knowledge discussed in this Unit are tied to very basic truths, as for example Carl Sagan's statement: "We are a rare, yet endangered species."

Although each of the three selections in this unit treats the search for knowledge quite differently, they are all concerned with the significant element which sets the human species apart. Unit Nine begins with an article about the quality of education in the U.S. in which the writer, educated in a traditional, Asian (colonial) culture, speaks out for the positive features he finds in the American system. Next is an essay by one of the leading social philosophers of the century, Bertrand Russell. When asked what had been the principles that guided him through his highly productive life, he mentioned three crucial elements without which, he said, he could not exist—one was the pursuit of knowledge.

The last selection is a passage from Carl Sagan's famous book *Cosmos* (which formed the basis for a popular television series), a visionary examination of how humans fit into the entire universe, or the broadest possible context in which the search for knowledge takes place.

All of the selections share the common theme that mankind can be preserved, first and foremost, by increasing knowledge through an understanding of its own potential for both creativity and self-destruction.

We Should Cherish Our Children's Freedom to Think

Pre-Reading Tactics

A. Read the **title:**

If *cherish* means "to value highly," what do you think the writer's message might be in this article?

B. What, in your opinion, should the main goal of education be? Check the one which represents your opinion.

1. To provide a good foundation in the basic skills such as reading, writing, and math.
2. To foster the acquisition of a large body of knowledge in a variety of academic fields.
3. To encourage the promotion of self-esteem and one's well-being.
4. To encourage and promote opportunities for creativity and self-expression.
5. To provide a firm basis for one to advance socially and economically.

C. Read the selection and compare your ideas about education with the writer's point of view.

D. Vocabulary Awareness—Learn the meaning of these **key expressions:**
Match words and expressions in A with meanings in B:

A	**B**
1. educational system	_____ something new or different
2. innovations	_____ school system
3. creativity	_____ the ability to express one's thoughts and feelings
4. meet high standards	_____ the freedom to speak openly
5. self-expression	_____ require a high level of performance
6. the license to speak freely	_____ being productive and imaginative

We Should Cherish Our Children's Freedom to Think

by Kie Ho

1   Americans who remember "the good old days" are not alone in complaining about the educational system in this country. Immigrants, too, complain, and with more up-to-date comparisons. Lately I have heard a Polish refugee express *dismay* that his daughter's high school has not taught her the difference between Belgrade and Prague. A German friend was furious when he learned that the mathematics test given to his son on his first day as a freshman included multiplication and division. A Lebanese boasts that the average high-school graduate in his homeland can speak fluently in Arabic, French and English. Japanese businessmen in Los Angeles send their children to private schools staffed by teachers imported from Japan to learn mathematics at Japanese levels, generally considered at least a year more advanced than the level here.

2   But I wonder: If American education is so tragically inferior, why is it that this is still the country of innovation?

3   I think I found the answer on an excursion to the Laguna Beach Museum of Art, where the work of schoolchildren was on exhibit. Equipped only with colorful yarns, foil paper, felt pens and crayons, they had transformed simple paper lunch bags into, among other things, a waterfall with flying fish, Broom Hilda the witch and a house with a woman in a skimpy bikini hiding behind a swinging door. Their public school had provided these children with opportunities and direction to fulfill their creativity, something that people tend to *dismiss* or *take for granted*.

4   When I was 12 in Indonesia, where education followed the Dutch system, I had to memorize the names of all the world's major cities, from Kabul to Karachi. At the same age, my son, who was brought up a Californian, thought that Buenos Aires was Spanish for good food—a plate of tacos and burritos, perhaps. However, unlike his counterparts in Asia and Europe, my son had studied *creative* geography. When he was only 6, he drew a map of the route that he traveled to get to school, including the streets and their names, the buildings and traffic signs and the houses that he passed.

5   *Disgruntled* American parents forget that in this country their children are able to experiment freely with ideas; without this they will not really be able to think or to believe in themselves.

6   In my high school years, we were models of dedication and obedience; we sat to listen, to answer only when asked, and to give the only correct answer. Even when studying word forms, there were no alternatives. In similes, pretty lips were *always* as red as sliced pomegranates, and beautiful eyebrows were *always* like a parade of black clouds. Like children in many other countries in the world, I ▶

dismay—concerned amazement

dismiss—consider unimportant

take for granted—accept without questioning

disgruntled—disappointed (with the results)

We Should Cherish Our Children's Freedom to Think—cont'd

simply did not have a chance to choose, to make decisions. My son, on the contrary, told me that he got a good laugh—and an A—from his teacher for concocting "the man was as nervous as Richard Pryor at a Ku Klux Klan convention."

7 There's no doubt that American education does not meet high standards in such basic skills as mathematics and language. And we realize that our youngsters are ignorant of Latin, put Mussolini in the same category as Dostoevski, cannot recite the Periodic Table by heart. Would we, however, prefer to stuff the developing little heads of our children with hundreds of geometry problems, the names of rivers in Brazil and 50 lines from "The Canterbury Tales"? Do we really want to retard their impulses, frustrate their opportunities for self-expression?

8 When I was 18, I had to memorize Hamlet's "To be or not to be" soliloquy flawlessly. In his English class, my son was assigned to write a love letter to Juliet, either in Shakespearean jargon or in modern lingo. (He picked the latter: his Romeo would take Juliet to an arcade for a game of Donkey Kong.)

9 Where else but in America can a history student take the role of Lyndon Johnson in an open debate against another student playing Ho Chi Minh? It is unthinkable that a youngster in Japan would dare to do the same regarding the role of Hirohito in World War II.

10 Critics of American education cannot *grasp* one thing, something that they don't truly understand because they are never deprived of it: freedom. This most important measurement has been omitted in the studies of the quality of education in this country, the only one, I think, that extends even to children the license to freely speak, write and be creative. Our public education certainly is not perfect, but it is a great deal better than any other.

Kie Ho is a business executive who now lives in the United States.

grasp—understand, perceive

Post-Reading Activities

A. Apply your understanding of the article:

Think of two different school subjects—history and mathematics. How would the acquisition of knowledge be different in the systems described by the following statements taken from the article?

1. We sat to listen, to answer only when asked, and to give the only correct answer.

2. Learners experiment freely with new ideas and express their own thoughts.

3. Learners memorize as much information as they possibly can.

B. Discuss, in a group, the different educational experiences each member of the group has had, comparing them with the ideas brought forward in the article.

C. List the advantages and disadvantages of the two main systems referred to in the article. Then **write** your own set of ideal goals for education which would ensure a continuing search for knowledge and promote innovations.

Second Selection
What I Have Lived For

Pre-Reading Tactics

A. Read the **title:**
The title looks like a question that has become an answer; something like "These are the things (what) I have lived for." As you can guess from the title, the article will try to answer the question.

B. Read the brief biographical note about Bertrand Russell. What style do you think a philosopher might use in writing? As you read, pay attention to the style and the choice of words.

C. Look for the **organization** of this selection. There are five paragraphs in it: the first gives a summary answer to the question raised in the title; the last presents an evaluation of the whole answer. Read the first and last (fifth) paragraphs before you read the whole selection.
1. Which three elements are essential in the answer:
   a. l ＿＿＿ ＿＿＿ ＿＿＿
   b. k ＿＿＿ ＿＿＿ ＿＿＿ ＿＿＿ ＿＿＿ ＿＿＿ ＿＿＿ ＿＿＿
   c. p ＿＿＿ ＿＿＿ ＿＿＿
2. Which of the three elements do you think will be stressed most by Russell?
3. What is Russell's final evaluation of his life (Paragraph 5)?

D. Read the whole selection, looking for the elaboration on the three main elements mentioned in C(1) above, in the three central paragraphs (2, 3, and 4) of this passage.

What I Have Lived For

by Bertrand Russell

1   Three passions, simple but overwhelmingly strong, have governed my life: the longing for love, the search for knowledge, and unbearable pity for the suffering of mankind. These passions, like great winds, have blown me hither and thither, in a *wayward* course, over a deep ocean of *anguish,* reaching to the very *verge* of despair.

2   I have sought love, first, because it brings ecstasy—ecstasy so great that I would often have sacrificed all the rest of life for a few hours of this joy. I have sought it, next, because it *relieves* loneliness—that terrible loneliness in which one shivering consciousness looks over the *rim* of the world into the cold *unfathomable* lifeless *abyss.* I have sought it, finally, because in the union of love I have seen, in a mystic miniature, the prefiguring vision of the heaven that saints and poets have imagined. This is what I sought, and though it might seem too good for human life, this is what—at last—I have found.

3   With equal passion I have sought knowledge. I have wished to understand the hearts of men. I have wished to know why the stars shine. And I have tried to *apprehend* the Pythagorean power by which number *holds sway* above the *flux.* A little of this, but not much, I have achieved.

4   Love and knowledge, so far as they were possible, led upward toward the heavens. But always pity brought me back to earth. Echoes of cries of pain *reverberate* in my heart. Children in *famine,* victims tortured by oppressors, helpless old people a heavy burden to their sons, and the whole world of loneliness, poverty, and pain make a mockery of what human life should be. I long to *alleviate* the evil, but I cannot, and I too suffer.

5   This has been my life. I have found it worth living, and would gladly live it again if the chance were offered me.

Bertrand Russell (1872–1970) received the Nobel Prize for literature in 1950. However, he is perhaps most famous for his work in theoretical mathematics and for his social activism. Together with Alfred North Whitehead, he published Principia Mathematica (1910–1913). Throughout his long life, Russell campaigned against war, most recently against American atrocities in Vietnam.

wayward—stubborn
anguish—agonizing pain
verge—edge
relieves—lessens, alleviates
rim—edge
unfathomable—cannot be measured
abyss—bottomless pit
apprehend—understand, comprehend
holds sway—stays steady
flux—constant flow
reverberated—repeated (sounds)
famine—extreme hunger
oppressors—those who rule unjustly by force
alleviated—reduced, lessened (see *relieve*, above)

Post-Reading Activities

A. Classify the following words under one of the three elements in the passage: ecstasy; finding answers; oppression; famine; joy; discovery (of how things work); despair; understanding; relief of loneliness.

      love   *knowledge*   *pity*

B. In paragraph 2 the word *love* (appearing in the first line of the paragraph) is referred to four more times by the pronoun *it,* and a fifth time it is repeated. **Find** these instances.

    1. _____   **3.** _____

    2. _____   **4.** _____

C. In each of the central paragraphs there is one key sentence which evaluates Russell's own achievements with respect to love, knowledge, and pity. Find the sentences. **Discuss** them in a small group.

paragraph 2_____

_____

paragraph 3_____

_____

paragraph 4_____

_____

Third Selection
The Great Library of Alexandria: from *Cosmos*

Pre-Reading Tactics

A. 1. It is important to understand the **wider context** of this selection before reading it. First, the passage presented here consists of eight paragraphs taken from the book *Cosmos* by Carl Sagan. (The book is related to the television series of the same name.) As such, this selection is taken out of its wider context, or the book. Therefore, the reader must adjust for certain gaps in the themes and thoughts presented. Yet the passage given here is a unit in itself.

2. As you read this selection, remember that Carl Sagan, a respected scientist, has been very active in sharing his scientific knowledge with the larger public of nonprofessional readers. One might say that it has been a special vocation for Sagan to popularize science for readers at large. (Unit Five introduced examples of popular science writing.) This selection presents a clear general message—knowledge can help us understand the potential that the human species has not only for creativity but also for self-destruction.

B. Read the **title** carefully. Do you know which library the title is referring to? It is the well-known library that existed between 300 B.C. until about 400 C.E. (Common Era) and which at its peak contained more than half-a-million volumes.

C. Notice that this selection does not include **key expressions** or glossing of words. You can read it and get the main idea without them. In the Post-Reading Activities you will work with the key expressions.

D. Read the whole selection. Look for two main ideas:
1. The point mentioned above: the human race has the potential for advanced creativity but also for self-destruction; and
2. The study of Cosmos requires efforts that are shared by all nations of this planet.

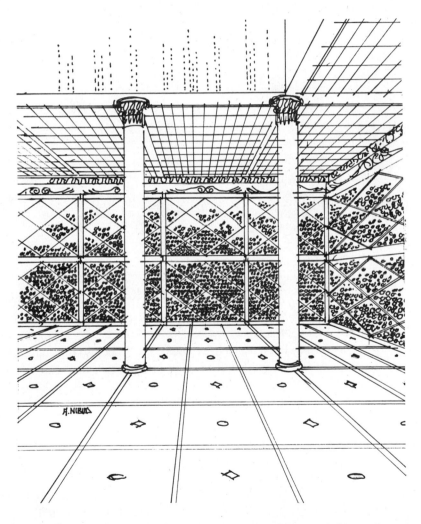

The library of Alexandria showing papyrus rolls, the "books" of the ancient world. An artist's sketch based on a reconstruction painting.

The Great Library of Alexandria

by Carl Sagan

1   There is no other species on Earth that does science. It is, so far, entirely a human invention, evolved by natural selection in the cerebral cortex. It is not perfect. It can be misused. It is only a tool. But it is by far the best tool we have, self-correcting, ongoing, applicable to everything. It has two rules. First: there are no sacred truths; all assumptions must be critically examined; arguments from authority are worthless. Second: whatever is inconsistent with the facts must be discarded or revised. We must understand the Cosmos as it is and not confuse how it is with how we wish it to be. The obvious is sometimes false; the unexpected is sometimes true. Humans everywhere share the same goals when the context is large enough. Present global culture is a kind of arrogant newcomer. It arrives on the planetary stage following four and a half billion years of other acts, and after looking about for a few thousand years declares itself in possession of eternal truths. But in a world that is changing as fast as ours, this is a prescription for disaster. No nation, no religion, no economic system, no body of knowledge, is likely to have all the answers for our survival. There must be many social systems that would work far better than any now in existence. In the scientific tradition, our task is to find them.

2   Only once before in our history was there the promise of a brilliant scientific civilization. Beneficiary of the Ionian Awakening, it had its citadel at the Library of Alexandria, where 2,000 years ago the best minds of antiquity established the foundations for the systematic study of mathematics, physics, biology, astronomy, literature, geography and medicine. We build on those foundations still. The Library was constructed and supported by the Ptolemys, the Greek kings who inherited the Egyptian portion of the empire of Alexander the Great. From the time of the creation in the third century B.C. until its destruction seven centuries later, it was the brain and heart of the ancient world.

3   Alexandria was the publishing capital of the planet. Of course there were no printing presses then. Books were expensive; every one of them was copied by hand. The Library was the repository of the most accurate copies in the world. The art of critical editing was invented there. The Old Testament comes down to us mainly from the Greek translations

made in the Alexandrian Library. The Ptolemys devoted much of their enormous wealth to the acquisition of every Greek book, as well as works from Africa, Persia, India, Israel and other parts of the world.

4   Alexandria was the greatest city the Western world had ever seen. People of all nations came there to live, to trade, to learn. On any given day, its harbors were thronged with merchants, scholars and tourists. This was a city where Greeks, Egyptians, Arabs, Syrians, Hebrews, Persians, Nubians, Phoenicians, Italians, Gauls and Iberians exchanged merchandise and ideas. It is probably here that the word *cosmopolitan* was realized in its true meaning—citizen, not just of a nation, but of the Cosmos. To be a citizen of the Cosmos . . .

5   Here clearly were the seeds of the modern world. What prevented them from taking root and flourishing? Why instead did the West slumber through a thousand years of darkness until Columbus and Copernicus and their contemporaries rediscovered the work done in Alexandria? I cannot give you a simple answer. But I do know this: there is no record, in the entire history of the Library, that any of its illustrious scientists and scholars ever seriously challenged the political, economic and religious assumptions of their society. The permanence of the stars was questioned; the justice of slavery was not. Science and learning in general were the preserve of a privileged few. The vast population of the city had not the vaguest notion of the great discoveries taking place within the Library. New findings were not explained or popularized. The research benefited them little. Discoveries in mechanics and steam technology were applied mainly to the perfection of weapons, the encouragement of superstition, the amusement of kings. The scientists never grasped the potential of machines to free people. The great intellectual achievements of antiquity had few immediate practical applications. Science never captured the imagination of the multitude. There was no counterbalance to stagnation, to pessimism, to the most abject surrenders to mysticism. When, at long last, the mob came to burn the Library down, there was nobody to stop them.

6   The last scientist who worked in the Library was a mathematician, astronomer, physicist and the head of the Neoplatonic school of philosophy—an extraordinary range of accomplishment for any individual in any age. Her name was Hypatia. She was born in Alexandria in 370. At a time when women had few options and were treated as property, Hypatia moved freely, unselfconsciously through traditional male domains. By all accounts she was a great beauty. She had many suitors but rejected all offers of marriage. The Alexandria of Hypatia's time—by then long under Roman rule—was a city under grave strain. Slavery had sapped ▶

classical civilization of its vitality. The growing Christian Church was consolidating its power and attempting to eradicate pagan influence and culture. Hypatia stood at the epicenter of these mighty social forces. Cyril, the Archbishop of Alexandria, despised her because of her close friendship with the Roman governor, and because she was a symbol of learning and science, which were largely identified by the early Church with paganism. In great personal danger, she continued to teach and publish, until, in the year 415, on her way to work she was set upon by a fanatical mob of Cyril's parishioners. They dragged her from her chariot, tore off her clothes, and, armed with abalone shells, flayed her flesh from her bones. Her remains were burned, her works obliterated, her name forgotten. Cyril was made a saint.

7   We have held the peculiar notion that a person or society that is a little different from us, whoever we are, is somehow strange or bizarre, to be distrusted or loathed. Think of the negative connotations of words like alien or outlandish. And yet the monuments and cultures of each of our civilizations merely represent different ways of being human. An extraterrestrial visitor, looking at the differences among human beings and their societies, would find those differences trivial compared to the similarities. The Cosmos may be densely populated with intelligent beings. But the Darwinian lesson is clear: There will be no humans elsewhere. Only here. Only on this small planet. We are a rare as well as an endangered species. Every one of us is, in the cosmic perspective, precious. If a human disagrees with you, let him live. In a hundred billion galaxies, you will not find another.

8   Human history can be viewed as a slowly dawning awareness that we are members of a larger group. Initially our loyalties were to ourselves and our immediate family, next, to bands of wandering hunter-gatherers, then to tribes, small settlements, city-states, nations. We have broadened the circle of those we love. We have now organized what are modestly described as superpowers, which include groups of people from divergent ethnic and cultural backgrounds working in some sense together—surely a humanizing and character-building experience. If we are to survive, our loyalties must be broadened further, to include the whole human community, the entire planet Earth. Many of those who run the nations will find this idea unpleasant. They will fear loss of power. We will hear much more about treason and disloyalty. Rich nation-states will have to share their wealth with poor ones. But the choice, as H.G. Wells once said in a different context, is clearly the universe or nothing.

Post-Reading Activities

Analyze each paragraph in order to understand the deeper meaning of this selection.

1. **Paragraph 1**
   a. A key issue which should concern all members of the human race, according to Sagan, is the question of human survival. In this paragraph he brings up several important facts which are related to this issue. Find the sentences in the paragraph that represent the following points: **Write** them on the lines below:
      (1) the uniqueness of the human race

      _____

      _____

      (2) some basic aspects of scientific research

      _____

      _____

      (3) the need for universal cooperation in cosmic research

      _____

      _____

   b. **Discuss,** with a partner, the full meaning of the following sentences which appear in the paragraph:
      (1) "There is no other species on earth that does science."
      (2) "There are no sacred truths; all assumptions must be critically examined."
      (3) "We must understand the Cosmos as it is and not confuse how it is with how we wish it to be."
      (4) "The obvious is sometimes false, the unexpected is sometimes true."
      (5) "And the study of the Cosmos provides the largest context."
      (6) "In the scientific tradition, our task is to find them (social systems)."

c. Consider the **meaning** of the following **words** as they appear in this paragraph. Choose the *best* equivalent from the three choices given below. Then compare your answers with your partner.

(1) *context*

   a) the situation or environment
   b) space
   c) time

(2) *sacred*

   a) precious
   b) expensive
   c) holy

(3) *consistent with*

   a) including
   b) in disagreement with
   c) in agreement with

(4) *discard*

   a) throw away
   b) write down on a card
   c) put down on record

(5) *revise*

   a) return to the original
   b) reexamine and change
   c) look at the facts again

d. **Discuss** with your partner how science can be misused.

2. Paragraphs 2, 3, and 4

a. Describe the city of Alexandria and the significance of the Great Library at its prime. Below is a list of ideas mentioned in these paragraphs. Find the sentences which describe these ideas.
Write them here. Then compare your answers with your partner.
(1) The Library was the center for the development of the sciences.

_____

(2) The Library was the center for the publishing and editing of the greatest books.

_____

(3) Alexandria was a truly Cosmopolitan city.

_____

b. **Discuss,** with your partner, what Sagan means when he uses the following expressions:
(1) ''the best minds of antiquity''
(2) ''the brain and heart of the ancient world''
(3) ''the repository of the most accurate copies in the world''
(4) ''exchanged merchandise and ideas''

3. **Paragraph 5**
   a. **Guess** the meanings of the words:
      (1) What prevented them from . . . *flourishing*
          (they could have developed but they didn't)
      (2) . . . the West *slumbered* through . . .
          (that period is called the "years of darkness")
      (3) . . . its *illustrious* scientists and scholars
          (these scholars were referred to earlier as "the best minds of antiquity")
   b. Sagan offers two possible answers to the question why the work of that period was lost. The sentences below contain Sagan's opinion. **Discuss** them with your partner.
      (1) The permanence of the stars was questioned; the justice of slavery was not.
      (2) The scientists never grasped the potential of machines to free people. Science never captured the imagination of the multitude.
   c. How is Sagan trying to prevent the same kind of destruction from taking place again?

4. **Paragraph 6**
   tells the story of Hypatia.
   Discuss, in a small group, the following elements of this story: (you and your partner join another pair to become a small group.)
   a. Hypatia's achievements for her time as a woman.
   b. The Christian Church fighting science as a sign of paganism.
   c. The sad fact that there was no one who would protect Hypatia and the Library.

5. **Paragraph 7**
   Discuss some of the differences and some of the similarities that you are aware of when comparing different cultures.

6. **Paragraph 8**
   Write answers to the following questions:
   a. What does Sagan mean by a humanizing and character-building experience? How does this relate to "We have broadened the circle of those we love"?
   b. Sagan emphasizes once more the need for a close sharing among the nations of the world. What does Sagan mean by that?

Unit Ten

. . . And Facing Death with Understanding

Background Information for Unit Ten

At some point, every person comes to terms with the finality of a single life by facing death. At first the prospect of dying might evoke anger, rejection, or avoidance on an individual's part; but eventually the inevitability of death must be confronted.

In this unit, you will read three selections in which writers relate various views of death. In the first two, young women write about the loss of someone close. In Selection I a sister describes her brother's death by cancer and how, living through that illness with him, she came to have a different view of her own strong, healthy body. Selection II is an account of a young man's suicide written by his best friend, the woman who must learn to respect his choice.

The author of the third selection, Elisabeth Kübler-Ross, is a psychiatrist who is widely known for her books and articles which stress each person's right—to the end—to be able to make choices about how one lives during the last period in life, as death approaches.

All three selections raise issues that can be the basis for examining your own personal and cultural experiences with death through the discussion questions which appear in the Post-Reading Activities.

A Sound Mind in a Sound Body

Pre-Reading Tactics

A. Read the **title:**

The key to understanding the writer's point of view lies in the meaning, in this context, of *sound body*. Do you think a *sound body* is:

1. a perfect body?
2. a terrific body?
3. a functioning and healthy body?

B. Vocabulary Awareness—These key expressions have different meanings for the author. Match each one with the correct description. Be sure to check your answers *after* reading the selection.

A	**B**
1. a perfect body	_____ a body which works well on the inside
2. a sound body	_____ the kind of body shown in TV commercials
3. a terrific body	_____ a body that is connected to a growing, expanding mind
4. a functioning and healthy body	_____ the body we think we should have so that other people will admire us.

C. Look for the writer's **point of view:**

1. As you read, look for the way the writer tells how and why she changed her own view of her body.

2. **Think about:**

   a. Is the writer more concerned with life or death?
   b. Does she feel angry about her brother's death?
   c. Does she reject the idea of his death?
   d. Does she avoid thinking about his death?

Developing a Sound, Striving Mind in a Sound Body

by Judy Lane McDaniel

1 I have a beautiful body. I'm not ashamed to admit it. It is one of the most splendid of specimens. I don't belong to a health club, I have a weakness for ice cream and cosmetic surgery *appalls* me. What's my secret and why am I so *smug* about it?

2 First, I must clarify something. After reading my first sentence, most people would envision an *egotistical* but nonetheless gorgeous creature, just like someone they saw in a magazine or perhaps in person at an Olympic event. That's not quite what I am talking about. The *true* perfection of my body is not obvious to the naked eye.

3 Like many young women, I was *plagued with* the insane desire to have the perfect body. The kind that belongs to those women who have so much fun in life, or so one would *surmise* from television commercials. And who, in between studying to be brain surgeons, are featured in men's magazines. Presumably along with that terrific body came success and total happiness.

4 I have difficulty admitting that I fell prey to the Madison Avenue criteria for beauty, but there is hardly a medium of advertisement or entertainment that does not thrust it upon us.

5 Recently, a series of events changed my feelings on the subject. My strong, beautiful, younger brother died of cancer at the age of 25. Over the past seven months, I observed the decay and ultimate destruction of his lovely structure and young life. The arm that once could handle endless repetitions with a 10-pound barbell could barely lift a cup to his lips. The powerful legs that passed me several times on the track could no longer balance his skeletal frame. In addition to unparalleled grief, I felt shame for having placed so much importance on such superficial ideals.

6 While *buying into* a commercial idea of what is beautiful, and by *virtue of exclusion,* what is not, I lost touch with what was really valuable. Until I was witness to the savage thievery of cancer, I never realized that there is nothing more beautiful than a functioning and healthy body, whatever its proportions. Sharing the frustration of his never-ending pain and constant battle to overcome his fate, I soon discovered that true beauty and strength can be seen and felt in a darkened room without benefit of the senses of sight and touch. I also learned that what's important is my own approval and acceptance of myself, not another's.

7 I have hardly stopped caring for my body. But now I do it more realistically and with a different purpose in mind. I am conscious of what I eat in order to maintain a more powerful immune system, not to force myself into a popular size. I employ the use of weights to remain strong, not to win a wet T-shirt contest. And the physical feats I may attempt are for my own satisfaction and do not require audience approval.

8 Amazingly, the effects are the same. My body is beautiful. Not perfect, beautiful—from the *inside* out. It functions properly, it allows me the freedom to do the things I want, and as a bonus my less-than-perfect mind is expanding and growing too. While I won't be found in the centerfold of any men's magazine, if the *AMA* wants a view of my lungs, digestive tract and circulatory system, I can be had for a price.

McDaniel is a free-lance writer.

appalls—causes dismay or horror
smug—self-satisfied
egotistical—too concerned with oneself; conceited
plagued (with)—to be tormented by
surmise—to believe without being sure
buying into—accepting
by virtue of exclusion—because of leaving out
AMA—American Medical Association

Post-Reading Activities

A. Find the time-line:

In this essay, the writer sketches three periods in her life. By doing so, she shows how she changed over time.

  Period 1: Before her brother died
  Period 2: During his illness
  Period 3: After his death

Fit the phrases below, which the writer uses to describe herself, into the time-line showing the periods in her life. Use the numbers of the phrases only.

Before	*During*	*After*

The numbers you place on the time-line should *not* appear in their order below.

 1. plagued with an insane desire for a perfect body
 2. finds that her mind is expanding and growing too
 3. fell prey to Madison Avenue criteria for beauty
 4. experienced unparalleled grief
 5. bought into a commercial idea of what is beautiful
 6. felt shame for placing importance on superficial values
 7. proud of not belonging to a health club
 8. hasn't stopped caring for her body
 9. realized she had lost touch with what is really valuable
10. attempts physical feats for her own satisfaction

B. Talk about these issues in a small group or with a partner.
  1. Is the writer mainly concerned with life or death?
  2. Do you think she would have changed if her brother hadn't died?
  3. Have you ever known someone who changed because of the death of a close relative or friend?

He Chooses Death—A Final Act of Bravery

Pre-Reading Tactics

A. Read the **title:**

1. The first phrase, *he chooses death,* is a headline; it gives the main fact of the article. The second phrase, *a final act of bravery,* offers an opinion about that fact; the headline makes a judgment. But that phrase, *a final act of bravery,* appears in Paragraph 12, almost at the end.

2. As you read, think about why the writer waits until the end of the essay to give an opinion on her friend's suicide.

B. Vocabulary Awareness—Learn these **key expressions:**

demons—evil spirits/devils
emotionally handicapped—has great limitations to function emotionally
torment—cause to suffer
to cope (with) anxiety—to be successful in dealing with, to manage

C. Look for the **organization:**

In this essay, the writer copes with her sense of loss following the suicide of her best friend. Her writing describes the stages she went through following his death.

As you read, look for the way her perspective changes as she moves through stages of anger, regret, denial, rejection, and finally acceptance of the choice he made.

D. You should be accustomed now to reading the entire selection without using your dictionary.

He Chooses Death—a Final Act of Bravery

by Joan Friedberg

1   I didn't see the note, but his father told me later that it simply said, ''I have decided to take my life.''

The man who had been my roommate, my lover and my best friend for the last 6 months had left and would never be back. His note to me had said, ''I had to leave today. I left fresh water and extra food for the cat.'' Oddly, he was more concerned about the cat's survival in his absence than his own. He was found the following afternoon by a maid in a motel in Tustin. Vodka and sleeping pills had cured his *chronic insomnia* for the last time.

2   For days following the news I asked myself the obvious: Why did he choose death when things were going so well for him? As a person who loves life and fears death, I have always wondered why anyone would willingly take his own life. And how could those around such a person let it happen? What had gone wrong?

3   Our friends, though sympathetic and supportive, responded with their own theories. ''I didn't know he was that disturbed.'' ''It must have been a moment of madness.''

4   Meanwhile, I sat alone trying to accept the impossible. I cried out loud to tell him one more time that I had loved him. But it was too late. He couldn't hear me now. But, just in case I was wrong and there was an afterlife, I asked my grandmother who died several years ago to look out for him. As I sat talking to ghosts, I realized that I had become the image of my mother's worst fears: living alone in an apartment with only one's cat for companionship and talking to oneself.

5   When my *composure* finally returned, I tried to sort out the past. I looked at his photograph, remembering that lock of blond hair that always fell across his forehead and his sometimes silly grin. Memories are painful. They go back to our first date, when he missed part of the film because he was waiting in the lobby to buy popcorn for me. They go back to the times when he would bring me coffee in the morning, or when he would write a few nice thoughts on a card. The times we walked together along the beach, his imitations of the old Honeymooner TV series with dialogue remembered word for word, the long serious talks into the night.

6   Our joys were not so different from those of most couples. But his sorrows were different, and perhaps there lies the answer. I sat reading his journal, trying to find the clues that I must have missed and that might have been a forewarning of his final act. I found that death had been with him for a long time. To him, the world was a hopeless mess. He was tormented by the thought that certain demons were trying to kill him. And, whether the demons existed in reality or only in his mind, he was right. They killed him in the end.

7   To those of us who are able to cope with *adversity,* it is difficult to understand a person who cannot. But, ▶

chronic insomnia—constant inability to sleep
composure—calm
adversity—bad times

just as there are people who are crippled in their bodies, there are others who are crippled in their emotional makeup. He wrote in his journal, "My personal destiny will soon self-destruct. That, from the very beginning, my destiny was like a puzzle with a deliberately missing piece was bearable to me. But society cannot tolerate *enigmatic* puzzles, however harmless." For the emotionally handicapped, the torment of living in a sometimes cruel world is unbearable. For them, the struggle to survive is a fate worse than death.

8 We were two *rebels,* both going against the tide. But, while I delighted in my *rebellion,* he stood firmly serious in his, a man against the world. I saw life's events as minor obstacles to be overcome, myself as the hero. He saw himself as a victim of treachery, a *martyr* to defeat. While I see little meaning in life, I still find a purpose in living. He wrote in his journal, "I know that the day is approaching when my personal sense of purpose will be tested to the core."

9 There were so many signs of hope. He had just started a new job. He talked of goals. He got a haircut, and bought two new pairs of pants. A part of him wanted to live, but something made him decide to give up what must have finally seemed to be a hopeless struggle.

10 My own shock and grief took possession of me for days after I heard the news. Food suddenly lost all taste; music and laughter seemed cruel to my ears. I've never wished so much that I could have had some control over another person's will. I've never been so sorry that I couldn't turn back the clock and play that last hand differently.

11 But I realize now that, in choosing death, he made a choice that was well thought out, planned, perhaps inevitable. It wasn't a cry for help. He methodically disposed of his belongings and put the house in order. He left no possibility open for anyone to save him from himself. Many of his journal writings indicate that he had long *flirted* with the idea of death.

12 For a person who has successfully coped with failure, the possibility of a bright future presents a frightening promise. It means coping in new ways, taking greater risks, having higher unrealized hopes. Perhaps his future was blindingly bright. "Do you know what happens to a moth when it gets too close to the flame from a candle?" his journal asks rhetorically.

13 Death was perhaps a better choice in his eyes. It offered a final escape from the despair that he so carefully tried to conceal. It held *bittersweet revenge* toward his enemies and eternal peace to him. It meant an end to the struggle, the torment, the anxiety, the fears. It was a second chance, a final act of bravery to be followed by a rebirth.

14 He and I saw life from two very different *perspectives.* And, while I would not have chosen his way out, only he could have lived his life. And he chose not to live it any longer. I've come to respect his choice.

enigmatic—mysterious

rebel (v.) rebellion (n.)—to be against the accepted order of things

martyr—a person whose death justifies his/her actions in life; arousing sympathy of others by dying

flirted—thought seriously about

bittersweet revenge—getting back at someone with pain and pleasure

perspectives—viewpoints

Post-Reading Activities

A. Interpret the writer's meaning: Psychologists have pointed out that people move through stages of behavior when they must cope with a personal loss such as death. One way to interpret the writer's description of how she dealt with her friend's suicide is to look for these stages in her words:

1. feeling angry
   (Why did this happen to me?)
2. feeling regret
   (Why didn't I say/do things I meant to?)
3. denying or avoiding the event
   (often by having fantasies)
4. rejecting or turning away from the event
5. finally accepting it, coming to terms with it

Scan to find these key phrases in the article that show the stages which the writer moved through until she was able to accept her friend's suicide. In a small group, **discuss** the question:

1. Paragraph 4
   "I cried out loud to tell him once more I love him."
   Do you think she feels anger? What else does she write that suggests she is angry with him?

2. Paragraph 10
   "I've never been so sorry that I couldn't turn back the clock."
   How does she express her regret? What things would she have said to him if he were still alive?

3. Paragraph 5
   "memories are painful"
   Why does she relate her fantasies about what they did together when he was alive? Is she denying or avoiding the reality of his death?

4. Paragraphs 7, 8, 9

''To those of us who are able to cope with adversity it is difficult to understand a person who cannot.''
What are the ways in which she compares herself with him? Is it a way of rejecting or turning away from the event?

5. Paragraph 12

''His journal (writing) asks: 'Do you know what happens to a moth when it gets too close to a candle'?''
(If you have forgotten what a moth is, scan back to the story you read in Unit Two.) Is she finally coming to accept his suicide? What other key sentences tell you that she has reached the stage of acceptance?

B. **Write** about your own experience with life:

The stages described in Part A also seem to take place when we must give up something very important and significant in our life: for example, losing one's job, not receiving an acceptance to a school of one's own choice, permanent separation from a familiar place when it is not your decision to leave. **Write** a composition in which you describe a significant event in your own life when you had a loss—you had to give up something. Use the outlines in Part A (1, 2, 3, 4, 5) as a guide for writing.

The Fear of Dying

Pre-Reading Tactics

A. Read the **title:**
Can you guess whose fear the title refers to? Is it one person's fear of
death, or does it refer to a universal fear? As you read, consider if the title
actually describes the main idea of the passage.

B. Review **familiar expressions** and learn **key ones:**
This selection contains words which should now be familiar since you have
found them in previous reading passages.

anger	anxiety
coping (dealing) with	dehumanized
siblings	depersonalized
acceptance	

C. Read **without knowing every word:**
Paragraphs 15 and 16 contain some medical terms that have not been
glossed. Even if you do not understand these words, you can still
comprehend the writer's viewpoint. In fact, in reading the passage, a
native speaker of English would probably not stop to check their meanings.

D. Read a **longer passage:**
With this final selection of Part II, you will be reading a passage that is
longer than most that have preceded it. Try to read for comprehension by
thinking about your own experiences in relation to the two situations the
author describes:
1. A man dies at home surrounded by his family.
2. A death in a modern hospital in which the patient is dehumanized by
   modern medicine.

The Fear of Dying

by Elisabeth Kübler-Ross

1   The ancient Hebrews regarded the body of a dead person as something unclean and not to be touched. The early American Indians talked about the evil spirits and shot arrows in the air to drive the spirits away. Many other cultures have rituals to take care of the "bad" dead person, and they all originate in this feeling of anger which still exists in all of us, though we dislike admitting it. The tradition of the *tombstone* may originate in this wish to keep the bad spirits deep down in the ground, and the *pebbles* that many mourners put on the grave are left-over symbols of the same wish. Though we call the firing of guns at military funerals a last salute, it is the same symbolic ritual as the Indian used when he shot his spears and arrows into the skies.

2   I give these examples to emphasize that man has not basically changed. Death is still a fearful, frightening happening, and fear of death is a universal fear even if we think we have mastered it on many levels.

3   What has changed is our way of coping and dealing with death and dying and our dying patients.

4   Having been raised in a country in Europe where science is not so advanced, where modern techniques have just started to find their way into medicine, and where people still live as they did in this country half a century ago, I may have had an opportunity to study a part of the evolution of mankind in a shorter period.

5   I remember as a child the death of a farmer. He fell from a tree and was not expected to live. He asked simply to die at home, a wish that was granted without questioning. He called his daughters into the bedroom and spoke with each one of them alone for a few minutes. He arranged his affairs quietly, though he was in great pain, and distributed his belongings and his land, none of which was to be split until his wife should follow him in death. He also asked each of his children to share in the work, duties, and tasks that he had carried on until the time of the accident. He asked his friends to visit him once more, to bid good-bye to them. Although I was a small child at the time, he did not exclude me or my siblings. We were allowed to share in the preparations of the family just as we were permitted to grieve with them until he died. When he did die, he was left at home, in his own beloved home which he had built, and among his friends and neighbors who went to take a last look at him where he lay in the midst of flowers in the place he had lived in

and loved so much. In that country today there is still no make-believe slumber room, no *embalming*, no false makeup to pretend sleep. Only the signs of very disfiguring illnesses are covered up with bandages and only infectious cases are removed from the home before the burial.

6   Why do I describe such "old-fashioned" customs? I think they are an indication of our acceptance of a fatal outcome, and they help the dying patient as well as his family to accept the loss of a loved one. If a patient is allowed to terminate his life in the familiar and beloved environment, it requires less adjustment for him. His own family knows him well enough to replace a sedative with a glass of his favorite wine; or the smell of a home-cooked soup may give him the appetite to sip a few spoons of fluid which, I think, is still more enjoyable than an infusion. I will not minimize the need for sedatives and infusions and realize full well from my own experience as a country doctor that they are sometimes life-saving and often unavoidable. But I also know that patience and familiar people and foods could replace many a bottle of intravenous fluids given for the simple reason that it fulfills the physiological need without involving too many people and/or individual nursing care.

7   The fact that children are allowed to stay at home where a *fatality* has stricken and are included in the talk, discussions, and fears gives them the feeling that they are not alone in the grief and gives them the comfort of shared responsibility and shared mourning. It prepares them gradually and helps them view death as part of life, an experience which may help them grow and mature.

8   This is in great contrast to a society in which death is viewed as *taboo,* discussion of it is regarded as *morbid,* and children are excluded with the presumption and pretext that it would be "too much" for them. They are then sent off to relatives, often accompanied with some unconvincing lies of "Mother has gone on a long trip" or other unbelievable stories. The child senses that something is wrong, and his distrust in adults will only multiply if other relatives add new variations of the story, avoid his questions or suspicions, shower him with gifts as a *meager* substitute for a loss he is not permitted to deal with. Sooner or later the child will ▶

tombstones—markers on graves
pebbles—very small rocks
embalming—a process of preparing a body for burial
fatality—an accident that results in death
taboo—a topic which is not openly discussed
morbid—refers to death
meager—very small

The Fear of Dying—cont'd

become aware of the changed family situation and, depending on the age and personality of the child, will have an unresolved grief and regard this incident as frightening, mysterious, in any case very traumatic experience with untrustworthy grownups, which he has no way to cope with.

9   We would think that our great emancipation, our knowledge of science and of man, has given us better ways and means to prepare ourselves and our families for this inevitable happening. Instead the days are gone when a man was allowed to die in peace and dignity in his own home.

10   The more we are making advancements in science, the more we seem to fear and deny the reality of death. How is this possible?

11   We use *euphemisms,* we make the dead look as if they were asleep, we ship the children off to protect them from the anxiety and turmoil around the house if the patient is fortunate enough to die at home, we don't allow children to visit dying parents in the hospitals, we have long and controversial discussions about whether patients should be told the truth—a question that rarely arises when the dying person is tended by the family physician who has known him from delivery to death and who knows the weaknesses and strengths of each member of the family.

12   I think there are many reasons for this flight away from facing death calmly. One of the most important facts is that dying nowadays is more gruesome in many ways, namely, more lonely, mechanical, and dehumanized; at times it is even difficult to determine technically when the time of death has occurred.

13   Dying becomes lonely and impersonal because the patient is often taken out of his familiar environment and rushed to an emergency room. Whoever has been very sick and has required rest and comfort especially may recall his experience of being put on a stretcher and enduring the noise of the ambulance siren and hectic rush until the hospital gates open. Only those who have lived through this may appreciate the discomfort and cold necessity of such transportation which is only the beginning of a long ordeal—hard to endure when you are well, difficult to express in words when noise, light, bumps, and voices are all too much to put up with. It may well be that we might consider more the patient under the sheets and blankets and perhaps stop our well-meant efficiency and rush in order to hold the patient's hand, to smile, or to listen to a question. I include the trip to the hospital as the first episode in dying, as it is for many. I am putting it exaggeratedly in contrast to the sick man who is left at home—not to say that lives should not be saved if they can be

saved by a hospitalization but to keep the focus on the patient's experience, his needs and his reactions.

14   When a patient is severely ill, he is often treated like a person with no right to an opinion. It is often someone else who makes the decision if and when and where a patient should be hospitalized. It would take so little to remember that the sick person too has feelings, has wishes and opinions, and has—most important of all—the right to be heard.

15   Well, our presumed patient has now reached the emergency room. He will be surrounded by busy nurses, orderlies, interns, residents, a lab technician perhaps who will take some blood, an electrocardiogram technician who takes the cardiogram. He may be moved to X-ray and he will overhear opinions of his condition and discussions and questions to members of the family. He slowly but surely is beginning to be treated like a thing. He is no longer a person. Decisions are made often without his opinion. If he tries to rebel he will be *sedated* and after hours of waiting and wondering whether he has the strength, he will be wheeled into the operating room or intensive treatment unit and become an object of great concern and great financial investment.

16   He may cry for rest, peace, and dignity, but he will get infusions, transfusions, a heart medicine, or tracheotomy if necessary. He may want one single person to stop for one single minute so that he can ask one single question—but he will get a dozen people around the clock, all busily preoccupied with his heart rate, pulse, electrocardiogram or pulmonary functions, his secretions or excretions but not with him as a human being. He may wish to fight it all but it is going to be a useless fight since all this is done in the fight for his life, and if they can save his life they can consider the person afterwards. Those who consider the person first may lose precious time to save his life! At least this seems to be the rationale or justification behind all this—or is it? Is the reason for this increasingly mechanical, depersonalized approach our own defensiveness? Is this approach our own way to cope with and repress the anxieties that a terminally or critically ill patient evokes in us? Is our concentration on equipment, on blood pressure, our desperate attempt to deny the impending death which is so frightening and discomforting to us that we displace all our knowledge onto machines, since they are less close to us than the suffering face of another human being which would remind us once more of our lack of *omnipotence,* our own limits and failures, and last but not least perhaps our own mortality? ▶

euphemisms—using indirect expressions instead of direct ones
sedated—under the influence of medication
omnipotence—having ultimate power, control of our destiny

The author of "Fear of Dying," Elisabeth Kübler-Ross (born in Zurich in 1926) did relief work in post-war Europe and practiced medicine as a country doctor in Switzerland. Her books, On Death and Dying, Questions and Answers on Death and Dying, Death: The Final Stage, *and her many articles on death and dying for contemporary magazines do not mean that she is preoccupied with morbid concerns; on the contrary, Kübler-Ross speaks for consciousness, for a moral and ethical consciousness, that respects the individual's right—to the end—to know and choose.*

Post-Reading Activities

Discuss these questions with a partner or in small groups:

1. How does the writer describe the differences between:
   a. a death at home
   b. a death in a modern hospital
2. Describe your personal experience with either of those two situations.
3. Do you think the situations are as clear-cut as the writer suggests? Is one all positive and the other all negative?
4. What taboos surround death in a culture or country with which you are familiar?
5. What euphemisms are used to talk about death?

Part

3 Reading to Learn Through Using Past Experience

Background Information for Part Three

Suppose you have read on an interesting topic and decide to find out more about it. The purpose of Part 3 is to present subjects you have already become familiar with through previous selections and to guide you into reading further about them. Thus, you will be increasing your background knowledge by using the strategy for learning called reading-in-depth.

The post-reading activities in Part 3 focus on learning tasks which are associated with schooling. Yet reading to learn is a purpose that goes far beyond taking courses and studying for examinations. In fact, it enables one to read for acquiring knowledge in ways that suggest the goals mentioned by Bertrand Russell and Carl Sagan in Unit Nine.

In Unit Eleven, on "Suicide," you are introduced to an essential library research tool, *The Reader's Guide to Periodical Literature,* which enables one to find topic references in periodicals (magazines). From its listings, we select an article from *Psychology Today,* then link that content with a relevant section from a textbook on sociology.

The unit on "Calendars" draws on two additional sources for reading to learn, the encyclopedia and the dictionary. You already have a superficial background on the subject of calendar construction from having read about the search for a so-called "perfect" method for keeping track of days and years in a popular science article. Now you will further your knowledge by consulting reference materials.

Next, consulting the *Reader's Guide to Periodical Literature* turns up a report on a lively research topic: what happened to dinosaurs? Taken from a magazine in which scientists describe their own and others' work to educated, but nonspecialist readers, the article presents counterarguments to some prevailing hypotheses.

Finally, in Unit Fourteen, you have a chance to learn more about Alexandria, Egypt, and its famous history.

Unit Eleven

Suicide

First Selection

Suicide in the South Seas

Pre-Reading Tactics

A. Locate **additional information:**

After reading about a young man's suicide (Unit Ten), you may have wanted to know more about the phenomenon. You can use *The Reader's Guide to Periodical Literature* to find listings for subjects and authors in more than one hundred magazines published in the United States. A page from the *Guide* that includes the listing for the topic of "suicide" is shown on the opposite page. To use the *Guide,* you must also refer to the key to abbreviations at the beginning of each volume. Thirteen articles are listed. Skim the descriptions given for each. Which *one* might report on suicide in another part of the world?

Suicide

See also

Right to die

Adolescents do not have to self-destruct. J. Renfro. *Educ Dig* 50:28-30 F '85

Cleveland school supt. shoots self to death; leaves letter behind [case of F. Holliday] por *Jet* 67:55 F 11 '85

Doc Holliday's death [suicide by Cleveland's black school superintendent] N Karien. por *Newsweek* 105:33 F 11 '85

Mother of suicide victim forms family help group [D. Holley's mother] *Jet* 67:24 Ja 14 '85

Our kingdom of death and teen suicides [threat of atomic warfare] R. Lawrence. *Christ Century* 102:92-3 Ja 30 '85

Probing a mysterious suicide at Lazard Freres [suicide of D. Davis] D. Dorfman. *N Y* 18:15 F 11 '85

School supt. kills self 13 days before insurance policy allows full payment [case of F. Holliday] *Jet* 68:11 Mr 25 '85

Suicidal preschoolers study by Perihan Rosenthal and Stuart Rosenthal] C. A. Bridgwater, *Psychol Today* 19:17-18 Ja '85

Suicide [teenagers] il *Child Today* 13:5 N/D '84

Suicide in the South Seas [study by Ruth Haynes] J. Folkenberg, *Psychol Today* 19:78 Mr '85

Teen Suicide (special section) *People Wkly* 23:76-8 F 18 '85

VW settles with family of exec who killed self (W.B. Brock's suicide related to lawsuit charging discrimination against blacks) *Jet* 7:30 Ja 21 '85

When his health deserted him: diet and fitness guru Nathan Pritikin turned to suicide. E Hoover il *People Wkly* 23:528 Mr 11 '85

B. 1. The passage from *Psychology Today* is a summary of original research which was published elsewhere. If you wanted to find the source for the information, where would you look for it?

2. The passage clearly and concisely summarizes a longer piece of research. As you read, consider how you would make it even more concise.

C. Vocabulary Awareness—Learn the meaning of these **key expressions:**

communal—belonging to the people of a community

precipitating—bringing about in a hurry

intervene—mediate

factors—contributing elements

distressed—upset

abuse—misuse

Suicide in the South Seas

by Judy Folkenberg

On Vanua Levu, second largest of the Fiji Islands, the suicide rate among Indian sugar-cane farmers is alarmingly high, far outstripping that of the native Fijians. Family conflict and the lack of emotional support are major precipitating factors underlying the suicides among these Indians, descended primarily from *indentured* workers brought to the islands from Calcutta and Madras between 1879 and 1920. Social worker Ruth Haynes studied police and medical records and found that for male Indians the annual suicide rate between 1979 and 1982 in one cane-farming district was 61 per 100,000, compared with 11.6 per 100,000 for male Fijians, which is close to the rate in the United States. The rate for Indian women was 71.9 per 100,000, compared with no suicides among Fijian women.

Haynes found especially high rates of suicide among Indian women younger than 30 years of age and Indian men older than 30. She notes that for young Indian women, suicide often follows marital or family conflicts. "Daughters tend to be undervalued in much of Indian society, and may even be seen as a *liability* . . . where they are reared by the parents only to be 'married-off' at some expense in their teens."

From marriage onward, the young bride becomes the property of her husband. Subject to her in-laws' whims until she bears children—especially sons—the young girl is virtually on trial. (According to Haynes, a number of married women who committed suicide had been *taunted* by in-laws about childlessness.) In these rural areas, the young Indian woman often cannot reach her family of origin when distressed and therefore receives no emotional support.

This contrasts sharply with the Fijian way of life, which remains traditionally communal and provides several support systems, including close relatives, men's or women's groups within the village and village elders who often intervene in family and marital disputes.

Indian men commit suicide because of chronic ill health or because of financial failure or shame about court actions. Younger men who fail to continue their schooling return to the family farm with *dashed* expectations and little hope of independence, since they are subject to their fathers' authority. According to Haynes, family conflicts preceded a quarter of male suicides and a violent undercurrent ran through many of the quarrels.

Sugar-cane farming *exacerbates* these shaky family situations. Cane farms are isolated, the labor constant all year long and "economic pressures in the form of land rent, loans to be repaid and payments for goods obtained on credit against harvest payment lead to constant anxiety," Haynes says.

Hanging was the method most often chosen by those committing suicide, but Haynes discovered that a sizable minority of the suicide victims chose a method that appears to be an increasingly popular one in Third World countries. From Thailand to Trinidad, records show that the abuse of the herbicide paraquat is a heavily favored method of suicide. One mouthful proves fatal. In Western Samoa, for instance, 1981 figures show that 35 out of 42 suicides were due to paraquat poisoning. Before the introduction of paraquat in the early 1970s, suicide was virtually unrecorded on that island group. Now the suicide rate for young men between 15 and 24 years of age is 94 per 100,000.

Haynes reported her findings in the British *Journal of Psychiatry* (Vol. 145, p. 433).

indentured—slavery that involves a contract
liability—something disadvantageous
taunted—to be teased
dashed—broken hopes
exacerbates—increases

Post-Reading Activities

A. Write a summary:
Follow the topic headings to write a concise summary of the article. Your summary should contain no more than ten sentences. Summary writing helps you retain the information you have read.
1. Suicide rates: male Indians in Vanua Levu (Fiji Islands); female Indians under 30
2. Explanations for differences between men, women
3. Effect of sugarcane farming on family tensions
4. Contrast of Fijian and Indian ways of life
5. Most frequent method of suicide
6. Abuse of herbicide

B. This article reports on suicide rates in a particular place (Vanua Levu). Where would you look for a more general article about suicide?
(Turn to the next passage for one such possibility.)

Textbook Passage/"Suicide"

Pre-Reading Tactics

A. Use the **whole context:**

1. This passage is taken from a textbook used in college sociology courses.

2. If you want information about "suicide," you must use the Index (at the back) to find specific pages. Look at the insert from the Index. What pages should you look for?

3. As you read the passage from the textbook, you will see a few, small
   numbers about the lines (paragraphs 1, 2, 4). These refer to Notes at
   the end of the chapter. In a textbook, facts and summaries taken from
   other authors' works are cited in footnotes or endnotes.

B. Vocabulary Awareness—Learn the meaning of these **key expressions:**
   (degree of) integration—level/extent of
   form of deviance—different from the norm
   isolation—separation from all others
   statistics—numerical facts
   detachment—separation
   sex ratio—the number of men as compared to the number of women

Suicide

1   Suicide refers to intentional self-destruction or self-killing. Although suicide is considered a major form of deviance in contemporary American society, social reactions to this form of behavior show wide variations from society to society and in different periods of human history. Various Oriental cultures have looked upon suicide with some *ambivalence* and under certain circumstances it is not highly disapproved. Among the Chinese, suicide was permitted for reasons of revenge against an enemy. In Japan, it was *expected* that a soldier would commit a form of self destruction known as hara-kiri rather than permit himself to be seized by the enemy. During World War II Japanese ''suicide divers'' received military decorations in rather elaborate ceremonies before their suicidal flights. Attitudes of Western Europe and American society are and have been strongly opposed to suicide. Disapproval of suicide has been generally the case for all peoples within the Jewish and Christian religions. In 11th-century England, suicide was defined as a crime as well as a sin. Throughout the medieval period and into relatively recent times suicide was punished as a *felony*. The suicide's body was denied burial in a Christian cemetery and the suicide's possessions were confiscated by the Crown. Similar penalties were put into effect in the New England colonies and remained until the early 1800's in Massachusetts. Attempted suicide was a crime in England until 1961 and still remains a criminal offense in North Dakota, South Dakota, and New Jersey.[4,7]

2   Statistics indicate that the rate of suicide within the United States was 11 per 100,000 population in 1970. This rate has remained fairly stable over previous years. The United States suicide rate in 1960 was 10.8; in 1961, 10.4; in 1962, 11.0; in 1963, 11.0 per 100,000 population. Suicide rates are comparatively high in various other countries. In the late 1960's and early 1970's suicide rates in Switzerland, West Germany, Czechoslovakia, Finland, Sweden, Austria, and Hungary exceeded 17 per 100,000 population. In other countries such as Italy, Spain, Greece, Ireland, suicide rates were less than 6 per 100,000 during the same period.[14]

3   Suicides in the United States tend to occur more frequently among males than among females. The sex ratio for suicide is approximately four to one. Older people commit suicide more frequently than do younger people. The relationship of age to increasing rates of suicide is direct and highly consistent. The rate of suicide among married persons is far lower compared to single, widowed, or divorced persons. In addition

among married persons, the rate of suicide is far lower among those couples having children compared to childless couples. Whites commit suicide far more frequently than nonwhites—particularly blacks. With respect to religion, Protestants tend to have a higher suicide rate than Catholics and Jews.

4   One of the most important studies of suicide was made by the French sociologist Emile Durkheim.[15] According to Durkheim, suicide could be explained in terms of a variety of social or group factors as they affected individuals. Durkheim felt that the likelihood of suicide was related to the degree of integration or involvement of individuals within groups or society. Specifically, suicide was more likely to occur in the extreme circumstances where individuals lacked adequate integration within groups or society or in instances where individuals were too highly integrated into society.

5   Durkheim classified three major types of suicide: egoistic, anomic, and altruistic suicide. *Egoistic* and *anomic* suicide characterized a weak attachment of individuals to groups or society. For Durkheim, *egoistic* suicide was a form of ''self-centered'' suicide. In this instance the individual lacks full participation within groups together with the emotional involvement which participation entails. Durkheim felt this could explain the higher rates of suicide among Protestants as compared to Catholics as well as the high suicide rates among unmarried individuals compared to married persons. Protestantism advocates ''free inquiry'' into the Bible and religious matters and the doctrine of individual salvation. Catholicism stresses theological interpretation of the Bible in matters of faith, and also salvation through ''the church.'' Durkheim thus reasoned that individuals of Protestant faith would experience more isolation and detachment and less integration into a church as a form of group or association.

6   The higher rates of suicide among Protestants which Durkheim found thus reflect basic weaknesses in social constraints over behavior (including the act of suicide) characteristic of Protestant religious groups. Likewise, unmarried people were not subject to the group ties and the social constraints of marriage and family life. Durkheim felt that the lack of attachments to others and greater emotional isolation among the unmarried was a prime factor in explaining their higher rates of suicide compared to married persons. On the other hand, *anomic* suicide is not the result ▶

ambivalence—feelings that are in conflict
felony—a category of crime that includes murder and burglary
egoistic—self-centered
anomic—from *anomie;* alienation of an individual

Suicide—cont'd

of a lack of close interpersonal or group relations but instead occurs as a result of a breakdown of the values and *norms* of the group or society *itself*. Thus higher suicide rates are often found during times of political crisis, or economic depression. *Altruistic* suicide occurs as a result of extreme integration into a group or society to the point where group norms and goals are the only things that matter. The individual identifies with and becomes so highly involved and committed to the group that he would willingly give his own life if the values and norms of the group so require. The practice of hara-kiri among the Japanese, or the self-destruction of a widow at her husband's funeral in India, illustrates this form of suicide.

group norms—group standards

Post-Reading Activities

A. Use your notes:

Complete the informal outline with facts from the passage. The outline gives topic headings. Either use the outline printed below or copy it on another sheet of paper. Then fill it in with the necessary details. The result will give you a set of reading notes for the passage, the type of brief writing one does in order to remember the important points in a text.

1. definition
2. wide variation
   a. U.S.
   b. Asia
     —China
     —Japan
   c. W. Europe
     —England
3. statistics
   a. U.S.
   b. other countries

4. statistics/U.S.
   a. sex ratio
   b. age
   c. marital status
   d. race
5. Durkheim's classification
   a. egoistic
      —definition
      —examples
   b. anomic
      —definition
      —examples
   c. altruistic
      —definition
      —examples

B. Use your complete set of reading notes to write a brief, factual quiz covering the important information in the passage. You may only write ten questions.

C. Work with a partner. Exchange quizzes. Write answers to your partner's quiz while your partner writes answers to yours. You may use your reading notes.

D. Check each other's quizzes. Talk about why you wrote each question. The paragraph numbers will help you locate specific information.

Calendars

Calendar: World Book Encyclopedia

Pre-Reading Tactics

A. Read **in-depth:**

After reading the selection "4,000-Year Search for a Perfect Calendar" (Unit Five), you may have asked yourself:

1. Why has it been so difficult to develop a perfect (accurate) calendar?
2. How were different calendars adjusted to the needs of the people using them?
3. What other interesting facts can one learn about calendars?

B. Consult **references:**

1. One way to answer the questions in A is to look up the subject "calendar" in an encyclopedia or in a large English dictionary. Encyclopedias contain short articles on specific subjects aimed at giving the reader the relevant information on that subject. Dictionaries contain definitions of words and concepts. A dictionary entry is brief while an encyclopedia provides more detailed information including historical facts and application to different fields. In both, the entry is listed in alphabetical order.

2. This unit contains a passage on calendars taken from the encyclopedia *World Book* and an entry under "calendar" taken from *The American Heritage Dictionary* of the English language. Begin with the encyclopedia selection. Scan the whole article, paying attention to the subtitles. Notice how many concepts are familiar to you from reading Unit Five.

C. Vocabulary Awareness—You probably know most of these **key expressions** from earlier selections. They will be useful in understanding this selection:

solar—pertaining to the sun
lunar—pertaining to the moon
discrepancy—the difference between two similar things (solar and lunar)
perpetual—continuing indefinitely
accurate—precise

To test yourself, fill in the blanks with one of the following key expressions: *solar, lunar, discrepancy, leap year, predominantly, perpetual, astrological, accurate, calendars, occurrence.*
The measurement of time has been important to man ever since he began to settle and cultivate the soil. The rise of cities and complex urban life meant that 1 _____ measuring of time was even more necessary. Early 2 _____, which noted the division of time into known units, were based on knowledge of the seasons, 3 _____ data and religious ideas.
Primitive man reckoned time by the 4 _____ calendar—the phases of the moon and planets. In Egypt, however, from the Third Dynasty (2780 B.C.) the priests produced a 5 _____ calendar based upon a year of 365 days. Their researchers also formulated a calendar based upon the 6 _____ of the Nile flood.
The Romans also used a 7 _____ solar calendar, but it was not well adjusted to the true solar year. In 46 B.C. Julius Caesar reformed the calendar by adding one day to each year every four years, thus making a 8 _____ year. There have been further adjustments which led to our present calendar, but the 9 _____ between the solar and lunar reckoning are still a problem. One of the most significant developments of modern calendars is the existence of a 10 _____ calendar which gives us accurate information on any date in our time.

D. Read the whole encyclopedia selection rapidly. You can understand the content of the passage by using your previous knowledge of the topic and of the key expressions.

E. As you read, look for the subtitles:

The Calendar Today
History

Use the section and subsection titles, too, as aids to faster reading. They are in boldface and italics: **Ancient Calendars** and *The Babylonians*.

CALENDAR

CALENDAR is a system of measuring and recording the passage of time. A major scientific advance was made when people realized that nature furnishes a regular sequence of seasons. The seasons governed their lives, determined their needs, and controlled the supply of their natural foods. They needed a calendar so they could prepare for winter before it came.

Before the invention of the clock, people had to rely on nature's timekeepers—the sun, the moon, and the stars. The daily apparent rotation of the sun provided the simplest and most obvious unit, the solar day. The seasons roughly indicated the length of another simple unit, the solar year. Early people were not aware of the fundamental cause of the seasons, the earth's revolution around the sun. But it was easy to see the changing position and shape of the moon. As a result, most ancient calendars used the interval between successive full moons, the lunar month, as an intermediate measure of time. The month bridged the gap between the solar day and the solar year.

The lunar month, we now know, is about 29½ days long. Twelve such months amount to about 354 days. This interval is almost 11 days shorter than the true solar year which has 365 days, 5 hours, 48 minutes, and 46 seconds. But a year of 13 lunar months would amount to about 383½ days, and would be more than 18½ days longer than the solar year. The 13-month calendar is even less suited than the 12-month calendar to measure the year. This discrepancy explains the confusion that has existed in the calendar for thousands of years, and still exists in some areas. People have no accurate way to keep the lunar and solar calendars exactly in step.

The Calendar Today

Most persons in the Western World use the *Gregorian calendar,* worked out in the 1580's by Pope Gregory XIII. It has 12 months, 11 of them with 30 or 31 days. The other month, February, normally has 28 days. Every fourth year, called a *leap year,* it has 29 days. But even this calendar is not quite exact enough. In century years that cannot be divided by 400, such as 1700, 1800, and 1900, the extra day in February must be dropped. The century year 1600 was a leap year, and the year 2000 will be one.

Our calendar is supposed to be based on the year Jesus Christ was born. Dates before that year are listed as B.C., or *before Christ.* Dates after that year are listed as A.D., or *anno Domini* (in the year of our Lord). Non-Christians often write B.C.E., for *before Christian era,* and C.E., for *Christian era.* See B.C., A.D., CHRISTIAN ERA.

The Church Calendar is regulated partly by the sun and partly by the moon. *Immovable feasts* include Christmas and such feasts as the Nativity of the Blessed Virgin. They are based on the solar calendar. Such days as Easter are called *movable feasts,* because their dates vary from year to year, according to the phases of the moon. The other principal movable feasts of the church year are Ash Wednesday, Palm Sunday, Good Friday, Ascension, and Pentecost.

The Hebrew Calendar, according to tradition, was supposed to have started with the Creation, at a moment 3,760 years and 3 months before the beginning of the Christian era. To find the year in the Hebrew calendar, we must add 3,760 to the date in the Gregorian calendar. The year 1980 in the Gregorian calendar is the year 5740 according to the Hebrew calendar. But this system will not work to the exact month, because the Hebrew year begins in the autumn, rather than in midwinter. During the winter of 1980-1981, the Hebrew year is 5741.

The Hebrew year is based on the moon, and normally consists of 12 months.

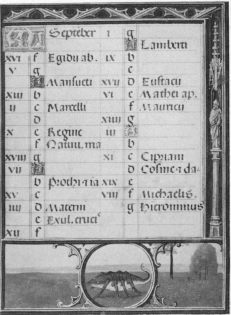

Detail from an illuminated manuscript. *The House of the Virgin* (1515); the Pierpont Morgan Library, New York City (Left) **A Flemish Calendar from the 1500's Shows the Month of September Illustrated with a Farming Scene (Right).**

These months are *Tishri, Heshvan, Kislev, Tebet, Shebat, Adar, Nisan, Iyar, Sivan, Tammuz, Ab,* and *Elul.* The months are alternately 30 and 29 days long. Seven times during every 19-year period, an *embolismic* or extra 29-day month is inserted between Adar and Nisan. The extra month is called *Veadar.* At the same time, Adar is given 30 days instead of 29.

The Islamic Calendar begins with Muhammad's flight from Mecca to Medina. This flight, called *the Hegira,* took place in A.D. 622 by the Gregorian calendar. The year is much shorter than the solar year, with only 354 days. As a result, the Islamic New Year moves backward through the seasons. It moves completely backward in a course of 32½ years. The Islamic calendar divides time into cycles 30 years long. During each cycle, 19 years have the regular 354 days, and 11 years have an extra day each. This method of counting time makes the Islamic year nearly as accurate as the year computed by the Gregorian calendar. The Islamic calendar would be only about one day off every 2,570 years with respect to the moon. The Gregorian calendar would be only a little more accurate with respect to the sun.

The Islamic year is based on the moon, and has 12 months, alternately 30 and 29 days long. These months are *Muharram,* ▶

CALENDAR—cont'd

Safar, Rabi I, Rabi II, Jumada I, Jumada II, Rajab, Shaban, Ramadan, Shawwal, Zulkadah, and *Zulhijjah.* The extra day in leap years goes to Zulhijjah.

History

Ancient Calendars usually represented some sort of compromise between the lunar and solar years, with some years of 12 months and some of 13.

The Babylonians, who lived in the southern part of the valley of the Tigris and Euphrates rivers, developed a calendar that represented many primitive procedures. They *intercalated,* or added, an extra month to their years at irregular intervals. When the royal astrologers discovered that the calendar had run badly out of step, they decreed an intercalary month. A calendar composed of alternate 29-day and 30-day months keeps roughly in step with the 354-day lunar year. To coordinate this calendar with the solar year, the Babylonians intercalated an extra month three times in a cycle of eight years. But even this did not compensate with sufficient accuracy for the accumulated differences, and the Babylonian calendar was quite confused.

The Egyptians were probably the first people to adopt a predominantly solar calendar. They noted that the Dog Star, Sirius, reappeared in the eastern sky just before sunrise after several months of invisibility. They also discovered that the annual flood of the Nile River came soon after Sirius reappeared. They used this event to fix their calendar, and came to recognize a year of 365 days, made up of 12 months each 30 days long, and an extra dividend of five days added at the end. But they did not allow for the extra fourth of a day, and their calendar slowly drifted into error. According to the famed Egyptologist J. H. Breasted, the earliest date known in the Egyptian calendar corre-

Embellished with 50 Engravings!

APPLEGATE'S
WHIG
ALMANAC,
For 1835.

NEW-YORK:
W. Applegate, Printer and Publisher,
No. 257 Hudson-Street.
ONE DOOR ABOVE CHARLTON-STREET.

Early Printed Calendars often had elaborate pictures. The American almanac shown above boasted 50 of them.

sponds to 4236 B.C. in terms of our present-day system.

The Romans apparently borrowed their first calendar from the Greeks. The earliest known Roman calendar consisted of 10 months and a year of 304 days. The Romans seem to have ignored the remaining 60 days, which fell in the middle of winter. The 10 months were named *Martius, Aprilis, Maius, Junius, Quintilis, Sextilis, September, October, November,* and *December.* The last six names were taken from the words for five, six, seven, eight, nine, and ten. Romulus, the legendary first ruler of Rome, is supposed to have introduced this calendar about 738 B.C. To make it correspond to the solar year, the Romans added a short month of 22 or 23 days every second year.

Politics soon crept into the calendar. One king added two months, *Januarius* and *Februarius,* at the end of the year. He hoped to collect more taxes during the extra months. Public officials used the months to stay longer in office. By the time of Julius Caesar, about 700 years later, the calendar was about three months ahead of the schedule fixed by the seasons.

The Julian Calendar. In 46 B.C., Julius Caesar asked the astronomer Sosigenes to review the calendar and suggest ways for improving it. Acting on Sosigenes' suggestions, Caesar ordered the Romans to disregard the moon in calculating their calendars. He divided the year into 12 months of 31 and 30 days, except for February, which had only 29 days. Every fourth year, it would have 30 days. He also moved the beginning of the year from March 1 to January 1. To realign the calendar with the seasons, Caesar ruled that the year we know as 46 B.C. should have 445 days. The Romans called it *the year of confusion.*

The Romans renamed Quintilis to honor Julius Caesar, giving us *July.* The next month, Sextilis, was renamed *August* by the Roman Senate to honor the emperor Augustus. According to tradition, Augustus moved a day from February to August to make August as long as July.

The Julian calendar was widely used for more than 1,500 years. It provided for a year that lasted 365¼ days. But it was exactly about 11 minutes and 14 seconds longer than the solar year. This difference led to a gradual change in the seasons. By 1580, the spring equinox fell on March 11, or 10 days earlier than it should.

The Gregorian Calendar was designed to correct the errors of the Julian calendar. In 1582, on the advice of astronomers, Pope Gregory XIII corrected the difference between sun and calendar by ordering 10 days dropped from October. The day that would have been October 5, 1582, became October 15. This procedure restored the next equinox to its proper date. To correct the Julian calendar's error regularly, the pope decreed that February would have an extra day in century years that could be divided by 400, such as 1600 and 2000, but not in others, such as 1700, 1800, and 1900.

The Gregorian calendar is so accurate that the difference between the calendar and solar years is now only about 26.3 seconds. This difference will increase by .53 second every hundred years, because the solar year is gradually growing shorter.

The Roman Catholic nations of Europe adopted the Gregorian calendar almost immediately. Various German states kept the Julian calendar until 1700. Great Britain did not change to the Gregorian until 1752, Russia until 1918, and Turkey until 1927.

Calendar Reform would simplify the present calendar. Three proposed calendars have received considerable support. In each, months and years would begin on the same day of the week and different months would have the same or nearly the same number of days. *The Thirteen-Month Calendar* would provide 13 months exactly four weeks long. The extra month, *Sol,* would come before July. A *year day* placed at the end of the year would belong to no week or month. Every four years, a *leap-year day* would be added just before July 1. *The World Calendar* and *The Perpetual Calendar* differ from one another slightly. But both calendars would have 12 months of 30 or 31 days, a year day at the end of each year, and a leap-year day before July 1 every four years.

DONALD H. MENZEL ▶

CALENDAR—cont'd

Related Articles in WORLD BOOK include:

Century	Equinox	Moon	Week
Christian Era	Hegira	Olympiad	Year
Day	Leap Year	Season	
Epoch	Month	Time	

CALENDAR STONE. See AZTEC (The Arts).

CALENDER is a machine that presses cloth, rubber, paper, and other material between rollers to make it smooth and glossy. See PAPER (The Processes; picture: How Paper Is Made); PLASTICS (Making Plastics Products; picture: How Plastic Products Are Made).

CALENDS. See MONTH.

1		2		3		4		5		6		7	
Monday	1	Tuesday	1	Wednesday	1	Thursday	1	Friday	1	Saturday	1	SUNDAY	1
Tuesday	2	Wednesday	2	Thursday	2	Friday	2	Saturday	2	SUNDAY	2	Monday	2
Wednesday	3	Thursday	3	Friday	3	Saturday	3	SUNDAY	3	Monday	3	Tuesday	3
Thursday	4	Friday	4	Saturday	4	SUNDAY	4	Monday	4	Tuesday	4	Wednesday	4
Friday	5	Saturday	5	SUNDAY	5	Monday	5	Tuesday	5	Wednesday	5	Thursday	5
Saturday	6	SUNDAY	6	Monday	6	Tuesday	6	Wednesday	6	Thursday	6	Friday	6
SUNDAY	7	Monday	7	Tuesday	7	Wednesday	7	Thursday	7	Friday	7	Saturday	7
Monday	8	Tuesday	8	Wednesday	8	Thursday	8	Friday	8	Saturday	8	SUNDAY	8
Tuesday	9	Wednesday	9	Thursday	9	Friday	9	Saturday	9	SUNDAY	9	Monday	9
Wednesday	10	Thursday	10	Friday	10	Saturday	10	SUNDAY	10	Monday	10	Tuesday	10
Thursday	11	Friday	11	Saturday	11	SUNDAY	11	Monday	11	Tuesday	11	Wednesday	11
Friday	12	Saturday	12	SUNDAY	12	Monday	12	Tuesday	12	Wednesday	12	Thursday	12
Saturday	13	SUNDAY	13	Monday	13	Tuesday	13	Wednesday	13	Thursday	13	Friday	13
SUNDAY	14	Monday	14	Tuesday	14	Wednesday	14	Thursday	14	Friday	14	Saturday	14
Monday	15	Tuesday	15	Wednesday	15	Thursday	15	Friday	15	Saturday	15	SUNDAY	15
Tuesday	16	Wednesday	16	Thursday	16	Friday	16	Saturday	16	SUNDAY	16	Monday	16
Wednesday	17	Thursday	17	Friday	17	Saturday	17	SUNDAY	17	Monday	17	Tuesday	17
Thursday	18	Friday	18	Saturday	18	SUNDAY	18	Monday	18	Tuesday	18	Wednesday	18
Friday	19	Saturday	19	SUNDAY	19	Monday	19	Tuesday	19	Wednesday	19	Thursday	19
Saturday	20	SUNDAY	20	Monday	20	Tuesday	20	Wednesday	20	Thursday	20	Friday	20
SUNDAY	21	Monday	21	Tuesday	21	Wednesday	21	Thursday	21	Friday	21	Saturday	21
Monday	22	Tuesday	22	Wednesday	22	Thursday	22	Friday	22	Saturday	22	SUNDAY	22
Tuesday	23	Wednesday	23	Thursday	23	Friday	23	Saturday	23	SUNDAY	23	Monday	23
Wednesday	24	Thursday	24	Friday	24	Saturday	24	SUNDAY	24	Monday	24	Tuesday	24
Thursday	25	Friday	25	Saturday	25	SUNDAY	25	Monday	25	Tuesday	25	Wednesday	25
Friday	26	Saturday	26	SUNDAY	26	Monday	26	Tuesday	26	Wednesday	26	Thursday	26
Saturday	27	SUNDAY	27	Monday	27	Tuesday	27	Wednesday	27	Thursday	27	Friday	27
SUNDAY	28	Monday	28	Tuesday	28	Wednesday	28	Thursday	28	Friday	28	Saturday	28
Monday	29	Tuesday	29	Wednesday	29	Thursday	29	Friday	29	Saturday	29	SUNDAY	29
Tuesday	30	Wednesday	30	Thursday	30	Friday	30	Saturday	30	SUNDAY	30	Monday	30
Wednesday	31	Thursday	31	Friday	31	Saturday	31	SUNDAY	31	Monday	31	Tuesday	31

A Perpetual Calendar will show the day of the week for any year desired. This calendar begins with 1753, the year after Great Britain adopted our present calendar. The calendar is easy to use. The letters after each year in the *Table of Years (on the opposite page)* refer to the first column of the *Table of Months (above)*. The figures given for each month in the Table of Months refer to one of the seven columns in the *Table of Days (above)*. For example, to find on what day of the week Christmas fell in 1900, look for **1900** in the Table of Years. The letter **a** follows. Look for **a** in the Table of Months, and, under December, you will find the number **6**. In the Table of Days, column **6** shows that the 25th day of the month, Christmas, fell on Tuesday in 1900.

	Jan.	Feb.	Mar.	Apr.	May	Jun.	Jul.	Aug.	Sep.	Oct.	Nov.	Dec.
a	1	4	4	7	2	5	7	3	6	1	4	6
b	2	5	5	1	3	6	1	4	7	2	5	7
c	3	6	6	2	4	7	2	5	1	3	6	1
d	4	7	7	3	5	1	3	6	2	4	7	2
e	5	1	1	4	6	2	4	7	3	5	1	3
f	6	2	2	5	7	3	5	1	4	6	2	4
g	7	3	3	6	1	4	6	2	5	7	3	5
h	1	4	5	1	3	6	1	4	7	2	5	7
k	2	5	6	2	4	7	2	5	1	3	6	1
l	3	6	7	3	5	1	3	6	2	4	7	2
m	4	7	1	4	6	2	4	7	3	5	1	3
n	5	1	2	5	7	3	5	1	4	6	2	4
p	6	2	3	6	1	4	6	2	5	7	3	5
q	7	3	4	7	2	5	7	3	6	1	4	6

YEARS 1753 TO 2030

	1786g	1821a	1856k	1891d	1926e	1961g	1996h
	1787a	1822b	1857d	1892n	1927f	1962a	1997c
1753a	1788k	1823c	1858e	1893q	1928q	1963b	1998d
1754h	1789d	1824m	1859f	1894a	1929b	1964l	1999e
1755c	1790e	1825f	1860q	1895b	1930c	1965e	2000p
1756m	1791f	1826g	1861b	1896l	1931d	1966f	2001a
1757f	1792q	1827a	1862c	1897e	1932n	1967g	2002b
1758g	1793b	1828k	1863d	1898f	1933g	1968h	2003c
1759a	1794c	1829d	1864n	1899g	1934a	1969c	2004m
1760k	1795d	1830e	1865g	1900a	1935b	1970d	2005f
1761d	1796n	1831f	1866a	1901b	1936l	1971e	2006g
1762e	1797g	1832q	1867b	1902c	1937e	1972p	2007a
1763f	1798a	1833b	1868l	1903d	1938f	1973a	2008k
1764q	1799b	1834c	1869e	1904n	1939g	1974b	2009d
1765b	1800c	1835d	1870f	1905g	1940h	1975c	2010e
1766c	1801d	1836n	1871g	1906a	1941c	1976m	2011f
1767d	1802e	1837g	1872h	1907b	1942d	1977f	2012q
1768n	1803f	1838a	1873c	1908l	1943e	1978g	2013b
1769g	1804q	1839b	1874d	1909e	1944p	1979a	2014c
1770a	1805b	1840l	1875e	1910f	1945a	1980k	2015d
1771b	1806c	1841e	1876p	1911g	1946b	1981d	2016n
1772l	1807d	1842f	1877a	1912h	1947c	1982e	2017g
1773e	1808n	1843g	1878b	1913c	1948m	1983f	2018a
1774f	1809g	1844h	1879c	1914d	1949f	1984q	2019b
1775g	1810a	1845c	1880m	1915e	1950g	1985b	2020l
1776h	1811b	1846d	1881f	1916p	1951a	1986c	2021e
1777c	1812l	1847e	1882g	1917a	1952k	1987d	2022f
1778d	1813e	1848p	1883a	1918b	1953d	1988n	2023g
1779e	1814f	1849a	1884k	1919c	1954e	1989g	2024h
1780p	1815g	1850b	1885d	1920m	1955f	1990a	2025c
1781a	1816h	1851c	1886e	1921f	1956q	1991b	2026d
1782b	1817c	1852g	1887f	1922g	1957b	1992l	2027e
1783c	1818d	1853f	1888q	1923a	1958c	1993e	2028p
1784m	1819e	1854g	1889b	1924k	1959d	1994f	2029a
1785f	1820p	1855a	1890c	1925d	1960n	1995g	2030b

Post-Reading Activities

A. Write a summary:

You noticed during your first reading that each section of the encyclopedia article is complete in itself. The first section explains what a calendar is and how it functions.

Follow the topic headings to write a brief summary of the first section of the article:

1. The function of a calendar.
2. The relation between time keeping and the seasons of the year.
3. Nature's timekeepers.
4. Lunar and solar measurements.
5. The problem of accuracy and discrepancy.

B. Complete the table below with information from each section:

Scan the sections describing the different calendars and complete the table below. This table should present the features of the three major calendars used today.

	The Gregorian Calendar	**The Jewish Calendar**	**The Moslem Calendar**
Beginning date			
Solar: yes/no Number of months			
Lunar: yes/no Length of months			
Leap year adjustments			
The name of the first and last month			
How widely used?			

C. Scan carefully the section dealing with "History." **Write** on one of the following topic headings to focus on some of the problems shared by all ancient calendars.

1. The need to rely on astrologers/astronomers.
2. The correction of errors of calculation.
3. Politics and the ancient calendars.

D. Study the section about the The "Perpetual" Calendar:

  1. Work on the example given in the explanation to the tables.

  2. Choose a date which has personal significance (past or future). Use the perpetual calendar to find the day of the week that event took/will take place.

  3. How important do you think the perpetual calendar is?

E. Skim the whole dictionary entry on "calendar" shown on pages 182 and 183. What information does the dictionary supply that does not appear in the encyclopedia? What information can only be found in the encyclopedia?

  Use the space below for writing notes.

  1. Compare your table from B above with the information given in the dictionary entry.

  2. Is the table with the months of the three major calendars (the way it is given in the dictionary) useful?

The dictionary:

The encyclopedia:

cal·en·dar (kăl′en-der) *n. Abbr.* **cal. 1.** Any of various systems of reckoning time in which the beginning, length, and divisions of a year are arbitrarily defined or otherwise established. **2.** A table showing the months, weeks, and days in at least one specific year. **3.** A list or schedule, especially one arranged in chronological order, as of cases on a court docket. **4.** *Library Service.* A chronological list of documents or manuscripts, usually annotated. **5.** *Obsolete.* A guide; example. —*tr.v.* **calendared, -daring, -dars.** To enter on a calendar; to list; schedule. —**Chinese calendar.** The lunar calendar of the Chinese, supposed to have begun in 2397 B.C. Years are reckoned in cycles of 60, each year having a particular name that is a combination of two characters derived schematically from two series of signs, the celestial and the terrestrial. Months are reckoned also in cycles of 60 that are renewed every 5 years, and each month consists of 28 to 30 days. —**ecclesiastical calendar.** A lunisolar calendar used in Roman Catholic and many Protestant countries, reckoning the year from Advent Sunday. —**Gregorian calendar.** The calendar now in use throughout most parts of the world, introduced by Pope Gregory XIII in 1582 and adopted by England and the American colonies in 1752. Also called ''New Style.'' —**Hebrew** or **Jewish calendar.** The lunisolar calendar used by the Hebrews, reckoning time from the year of creation, 3761 B.C., and based on a metonic cycle of 19 years, with the 3rd, 6th, 8th, 11th, 14th, 17th, and 19th years of each cycle designated leap years. —**Hindu calendar.** The lunisolar calendar of the Hindus, believed to date in its modern form from A.D. 400. The solar year is divided into 12 months in accordance with the successive entrances of the sun into the signs of the zodiac, the months varying in length from 29 to 32 days.

—**Julian calendar.** The calendar prescribed by Julius Caesar, introduced in 46 B.C. and replaced in most countries by the Gregorian calendar. Also called ''Old Style.'' —**Moslem calendar.** The calendar used in Moslem countries reckoning time from July 16, A.D. 622, the day after the Hegira, based on a cycle of 30 years, 19 of which have 354 days each and 11 of which are leap years, having 355 days each. —**Revolutionary calendar.** The calendar introduced in France on October 24, 1793, by the National Convention and abolished under Napoleon on December 31, 1805, reckoning time from September 22, 1792, the date of the founding of the First Republic. —**Roman calendar.** An ancient Roman lunar calendar designating the day of the new moon as the **calends** *(see),* the day of the full moon as the **ides** *(see),* and the ninth day before the ides as the **nones** *(see).* [Middle English *calender,* from Norman French, from Medieval Latin *kalendārium,* from Latin, a moneylender's account book (because the monthly interest was due on the calends), from *kalendae,* the CALENDS.]

cal·en·der (kăl′en-der) *n.* A machine in which paper or cloth is made smooth and glossy by being pressed through rollers. —*tr.v.* **calendered, -dering, -ders.** To press in a calender. [French *calendre,* from Medieval Latin *calendra, celendra,* from Latin *cylindrus,* cylinder, roller, from Greek *kulindros,* from *kulindein,* to roll. See **skel-³** in Appendix.*] —**cal′en·der·er** *n.*

ca·len·dri·cal (ke-lĕn′drĭ-kel) *adj.* Of, pertaining to, or used in a calendar.

cal·ends (kăl′endz) *n., pl.* **calends.** Also **kal·ends.** In the ancient Roman calendar, the day of the new moon and the first day of the month. [Middle English *kalendes,* from Latin *kalendae.* See **kel-³** in Appendix.*] —**ca·len′dal** (ke-lĕn′del) *adj.*

Months of Three Principal Calendars

Gregorian		Hebrew Months correspond approximately to those in parentheses		Moslem Beginning of year retrogresses through the solar year of the Gregorian calendar	
name	number of days	name	number of days	name	number of days
January	31	Tishri (September-October)	30	Muharram	30

February
  in leap year
	28
	29
		Heshvan
		  in some years
		(October-November)
			29
			30
				Safar	29

March	31	Kislev in some years (November-December)	29 30	Rabi I	30
April	30	Tevet (January-February)	29	Rabi II	29
May	31	Shevat (January-February)	30	Jumada I	30
June	30	Adar* in leap year (February-March)	29 30	Jumada II	29
July	31	Nisan (March-April)	30	Rajab	30
August	31	Iyar (April-May)	29	Sha'ban	29
September	30	Sivan (May-June)	30	Ramadan	30
October	31	Tammuz (June-July)	29	Shawwal	29
November	30	Av (July-August)	30	Dhu'l-Qa dah	30
December	31	Elul (August-September)	29	Dhu'l-Hijja in leap year	29 30

*Adar is followed in leap year by the intercalary month Veadar or Adar Sheni, having 29 days.

Dinosaurs

Selection
The Dinosaur Massacre

Pre-Reading Tactics

A. 1. Read **in-depth:**

When you read about dinosaurs in Unit Five, your imagination might have been caught by the fascinating question: what ever happened to them? Reading "Turtle May Be Clue to Dinosaur Demise" might have made you want to know more about the asteroid theory.

2. On the top of page 185 is the listing on "dinosaurs" from a fairly current volume of *The Reader's Guide to Periodical Literature*. Use this selection to answer these questions:

a. How many entries are shown for "dinosaurs"?

_____

b. Which of the entries could refer to the disappearance of dinosaurs?

_____

c. Of the possible references about the disappearance of dinosaurs, which ones appear in magazines that specialize in science? (Try to guess, even though most of the titles are abbreviated.)

_____

d. Which entries might give additional information about the asteroid theory?

_____

e. Which reference do you believe would give the most thorough information about the asteroid theory? Why?

_____

Dinosaurs

Debunking dinosaur myths [views of E. Colbert] F. Golden. il por *Time* 122:57 O 17 '83

Dinosaur ancestors unearthed in Texas. il *Sci News* 124:357 D 3 '83

Dinosaur death: with a whimper, not a bang [research by Robert Sloan] il *USA Today* 111:7-8 Je '83

The dinosaur massacre: a double-barreled mystery [refuting L. Alvarez's theory of asteroid impact as cause of Cretaceous-Tertiary extinctions: with editorial comment by Scott DeGarmo] R. Jastrow. il por maps *Sci Dig* 91:8, 50-3+ S '83

Dinosaur story: who found the tooth? [claim of Gideon Mantell] C. Simon. *Sci News* 124:312 N 12 '83

Dinosaurs overdosed into oblivion? [theory of Donald K. Siegel] J. Greenberg. *Sci News* 124:300 N 5 '83

Bibliography

Dinosaurs galore [books for children] G. McHargue. *N Y Times Book Rev* 88:46 N 13 '83

3. You did a good job if you selected the entry titled "The Dinosaur Massacre" by Robert Jastrow. Next, you will be able to read it.

B. Vocabulary Awareness—Learn the meaning of these **key expressions:**

validity—well proven arguments

evidence (physical)—proof that scientists find

interpretation—the meaning given to findings (by researchers and scientists)

(is) attested to—give evidence

speculation—conjecture/hypothesis

A. NIBUD

The Dinosaur Massacre: A Double-Barreled Mystery

by Robert Jastrow

1 Now and then a scientist stumbles across a fact that seems to solve one of the great mysteries of science overnight. Such unexpected discoveries are rare. When they occur, the scientific community gets very excited.

2 But excitement is not the best barometer of scientific validity. Science, said Adam Smith, should be "the great antidote to the poison of enthusiasm." The case of the disappearing dinosaurs is a fascinating demonstration that science is not based on facts alone. The interpretation of the facts is even more important.

3 Everyone knows the dinosaurs vanished 65 million years ago. The suddenness of their disappearance suggests that they were wiped out by some natural disaster. What was this catastrophe?

(Subtitle 1)

4 One possibility is a supernova—an exploding star that showered the Earth with lethal particles and radiation. Another possibility is a collision with a comet. A third idea is that an asteroid hit the Earth. The asteroid theory is more attractive than the others because many asteroids have orbits that cross the orbit of the Earth. Some of these asteroids are quite large, and once in a while one of the big ones collides with the Earth. Erosion and floods of lava tend to cover up the crater formed by the impact on the Earth, although on the moon many signs of past impacts are still visible.

5 A calculation on the back of an envelope shows that a large asteroid hits the Earth every 100 million years, on the average. That nearly happened in 1937, when Hermes, a rock the size of Manhattan Island, came within 400,000 miles of our planet—about as close as a celestial near-miss can be. A collision with the asteroid would have been traumatic. If Hermes had landed in the ocean, tidal waves would have raced around the globe, inundating coastal areas on many continents. If on land, devastating earthquakes would have resulted. Dust from the impact would have darkened the sky for months, killing many plants and breaking the food chain. Life would have been *decimated*.

6 The idea is a good one, and it has been kicking around for years. The trouble with it is that as a dinosaur-killer, an asteroid collision is pure speculation; no one has been able to find proof that such a collision actually occurred.

7 Imagine the *ripples* of surprise that spread through the scientific community when Luis Alvarez,

Nobel laureate in physics, announced he had discovered physical evidence—something you could actually hold in your hand—for the collision of a giant asteroid with the Earth exactly 65 million years in the past. The coincidence was overwhelming. Professor Alvarez, it seemed, had found the *smoking gun*.

8 What was the new evidence? Alvarez and his co-workers had analyzed the chemical ingredients of ancient rocks that lay on the floor of the ocean many millions of years ago. The rocks had hardened from the *ooze* made up of fine particles and the debris of countless dead organisms which accumulates on the ocean floor. Most of these rocks are buried deep under the present ocean floor, but in a few places on the Earth, the old rocks have been raised up and tilted, exposing the record of past accumulations. In these places, the layers of ancient ocean floor are clearly visible, stacked one on top of another like layers in a cake.

9 For his analysis, Alvarez picked a particular layer of rock known to be about 65 million years old. That is, it had formed from ooze that was lying on the ocean floor just around the time the dinosaurs disappeared. He found that this layer contained an unusually large amount of a rare metal called iridium.

10 What was the significance of this finding? The Alvarez team had the answer. Iridium is 100,000 times more abundant in meteorites that it is in the rocks of the Earth's crust. If a giant asteroid hit the Earth 65 million years ago, the dust cloud from the collision would be unusually rich in iridium. The dust cloud, blocking the rays of the sun for many months, would have caused the death of many plants; perhaps all plant life would have died. Without their normal diet of swamp greens, the plant-eating dinosaurs would have starved to death. The meat-eating dinosaurs, which normally dined on the plant-eaters, would soon have followed them into *oblivion*. A layer of iridium-rich dust, settling to the floor of the ocean, would have recorded the incident. Hardened into rock, it lay there until the Alvarez team unlocked its secret. ▶

decimated—(they) were killed off
ripples—small waves
smoking gun—the evidence that provides proof (or proof of the guilty person)
ooze—wet mud
oblivion—no longer in existence

The Dinosaur Massacre: A Double-Barreled Mystery—cont'd

(Subtitle 2)

11   The Alvarez theory has received wide acclaim from scientists. The physical evidence for it is compelling, and the reasoning has a clean and rigorous quality, as physicists' arguments usually do. But in truth, the Alvarez argument started to come unglued almost immediately on a simple point.

12   If an asteroid really did kill off the dinosaurs and other living organisms, the fossil record should reveal that fact; at a certain point in the record of the rocks, the remains of many plants and animals should disappear abruptly and simultaneously, all over the world. What does the record show? Paleobotanist Leo Hickey pointed out that many kinds of plants did become extinct around the time of the dinosaurs' demise, but their disappearance was gradual, persisting over millions of years. Furthermore, the plants disappeared at different times in different places. This picture was as far as could be imagined from the idea of a global catastrophe that killed plants all over the world at the same time.

13   The record on the extinctions of other animals showed that most kinds of animals also disappeared in a gradual way, rather than suddenly. That seems to have been true of the dinosaurs as well. These magnificent animals once roamed over the land areas of the world, but by the time of the supposed asteroid impact they had *dwindled* to no more than 20 species, living in North America along the shores of a *shallow* sea that covered what is now the northwestern United States. It appears that 65 million years ago, the dinosaurs were already on the way out; all the asteroid could have done was to polish off the few that remained in North America.

14   Still, there was the smoking gun—the iridium layer. That was a clear indication that a giant asteroid had hit the Earth. Surely the collision would have had a damaging effect on the life of the planet. But recent research suggests that the iridium layer was misinterpreted; there may not be a connection after all between the iridium layer and an asteroid impact.

● ● ●

(The original article cites research findings of the following scientists: Robert Reynolds and Michael Rampino; an Italian team of scientists; Charles Officer and Charles Drake, and Everett Lindsay, Robert Butler and Noyce Johnson in New Mexico. The sections detailing these researchers work have been cut to aid reading comprehension of the main ideas.)

● ● ●

The dinosaur bones do not disappear when the iridium layer appears; instead, they continue on well into the next magnetic zone, and persist long after the formation of the layer.

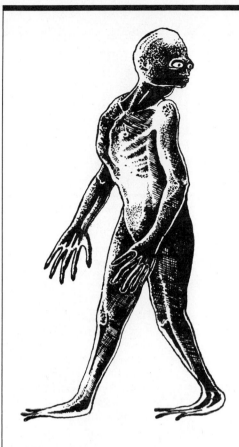

If the dinosaurs hadn't disappeared, they might have become bipedal, big-brained animals that looked something like this, according to paleontologist Dale Russell. These reptilian humanoids would probably have occupied the niche that man now does. A likely candidate for such development was Stenonychosaurus inequalus, a 10-foot dinosaur that had a brain-to-body ratio approaching that of primitive mammals.

(Subtitle 3)

15 So there we are. The asteroid theory was very attractive because it explained so much in a simple way, and many people will regret its passing. However, the evidence against it is very strong. That leaves the question: What did kill the dinosaurs? The answer is probably the one some paleontologists have suspected all along. The dinosaurs evolved during a long period of mild and constant climate that lasted more than 100 million years. During much of that period, a shallow sea covered part of North America from Canada to the Gulf of Mexico. Swampy lowlands and marshy terrain adjoined the sea; their presence is attested to by thick coal beds from Montana to northern New Mexico. The elements of that moist, clement world were in perfect balance for the dinosaurs; the plant-eating dinosaurs ate the lush vegetation, and the carnivorous dinosaurs ate the plant-eaters.

16 Around 80 million years ago, the sea covering western North America began to withdraw. As the waters *receded* and the continents became exposed, the climate of the world grew cooler and drier, and the vegetation became less abundant. Around 65 million years ago, the withdrawal of the waters accelerated; they receded rapidly ▶

dwindled—became smaller
shallow—not deep
receded—moved back

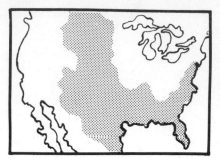

Did shrinking seas lead to the demise of the dinosaurs? During their reign, much of what is now the western United States was covered by water (above). This sea began to withdraw about 80 million years ago.

About 65 million years ago, around the time that the dinosaurs vanished, the shallow sea receded abruptly. Within 5 million years, the water had almost completely retreated (above).

toward the Gulf of Mexico; a few more million years, and the North American sea was gone. This change in sea level, which eliminated the habitat of the dinosaurs, provides a *likely* explanation for their disappearance.

17   The smaller varieties of reptiles, particularly the snakes and lizards, survived in the new era. A small reptile can crawl under a rock in the heat of summer and hibernate in the winter; but Tyrannosaurus and its kin were too big for that. When the environment changes drastically, animals adapted to the past cannot cope, and they become extinct. More than 90 percent of all the life forms that have ever lived on Earth have disappeared without leaving direct descendants. And so the problem of the dinosaur extinction has become a nonproblem. "Extinction," as paleontologist Thomas Schopf says, "is the normal way of life."

Robert Jastrow, founder and former director of NASA's Goddard Institute for Space Studies, is a geologist, an astronomer and a physicist.

likely—possible

Post-Reading Activities

A. Guide yourself to read the passage by groups of paragraphs:

Paragraphs 1–3
1. Establish motivation for reading the article; present the central problem.

Paragraphs 4–10
2. Present the asteroid theory supported by Luis Alvarez' evidence.

Paragraphs 11–14
3. Give the counter-evidence.

Paragraphs 15–17
4. Propose an alternative theory.

B. Discuss with a partner:
For each group of paragraphs, find several key sentences that are evidence for the organization in Part A (above).

C. Notice there is a large space and a line to write on before paragraphs 4, 11, and 15. Write subtitles that describe the paragraphs to follow.

(before paragraphs 4-10)

subtitle 1 _____
(before paragraphs 11-14)

subtitle 2 _____
(before paragraphs 15-17)

subtitle 3 _____

D. In a group, compare and discuss your subtitles.

E. Use a current issue of the *Reader's Guide to Periodical Literature* to find other articles about the disappearance of the dinosaurs. Why do you think the question is still alive?

Hypatia and Alexandria

First and Second Selections

Special References

Pre-Reading Tactics

A. Use specialized **references:**

Along with dictionaries, the *Reader's Guide,* and encyclopedias, there are hundreds of reference books in which one can locate specialized information. School, college, and public libraries keep reference books for use within the library.

Suppose you wanted to know more about the fascinating woman scientist, Hypatia, whose story Carl Sagan told in *Cosmos* (Unit Nine, Selection Three). A good place to look would be in a dictionary of biography which contains listings of famous people who are prominent in the sciences.

B. Use your previous **knowledge:**

Selections One and Two about Hypatia are from an encyclopedia and the *Dictionary of Scientific Biography.* You should be able to read them easily since most of the names of people and places are familiar. Do you remember?

People	**Places**
Hypatia	Alexandria
the Ptolemy kings	Egypt
Orestes	the library of Alexandria
Cyril	
the early Christians	
pagans	
Alexander the Great	

In reading Selections One and Two, you can expect to find new names of people, places, and events as well.

HYPATIA, hī-pā′shē-ə, Greek philosopher of the 5th century A.D., was perhaps the most famous woman philosopher in history. She was the daughter of Theon, a celebrated Alexandrian mathematician. Renowned for her beauty, modesty, learning, and eloquence, she became probably the most important figure in the Neoplatonic school in Alexandria, where she was said to support Orestes, the pagan prefect of Egypt, in his political opposition to St. Cyril, patriarch of Alexandria.

Scandalous stories about her friendship with Orestes, as well as disapproval of her non-Christian beliefs, eventually caused her tragic end. In March 415 a Christian mob in Alexandria, incited by fanatical clergy, stopped her carriage one day, carried her into the Church of the Caesareum, tore her limb from limb, and burned her broken body in the street. She is the heroine of Charles Kingsley's historical novel *Hypatia* (1853).

HYPATIA (*b.* Alexandria, Egypt, *ca.* 370; *d.* Alexandria, 415), *mathematics, philosophy.*

Hypatia, the first woman in history to have lectured and written critical works on the most advanced mathematics of her day, was the daughter and pupil of the mathematician Theon of Alexandria. It is believed that she assisted him in writing his eleven-part treatise on Ptolemy's *Almagest* and possibly in formulating the revised and improved version of Euclid's *Elements* that is the basis of all modern editions of the work. According to Suidas she composed commentaries not only on the *Almagest* but also on Diphantus' *Arithmetica* and Apollonius' *Conic Sections*. None of them survives.

Although accurate documentation of Hypatia's activities is lacking, it is known that she lectured in her native city on mathematics and on the Neoplatonic doctrines of Plotinus and Iamblichus and that about A.D. 400 she became head of the Neoplatonic school in Alexandria. Her classes attracted many distinguished men, among them Synesius of Cyrene, later bishop of Ptolemais. Several of his letters to Hypatia are extant. They are full of chivalrous admiration and reverence. In one he asks her how to construct an astrolabe and a hydroscope.

In spite of her association with Synesius and other Christians, Hypatia's Neoplatonic philosophy and the freedom of her ways seemed a pagan influence to the Christian community of Alexandria. Prejudice was strengthened by her friendship with Orestes, Roman prefect of the city and political enemy of Cyril, bishop of Alexandria. The mounting hostility culminated in her murder by a fanatic mob. None of her writings was preserved; but the general loss of Hellenic sources must be blamed on repeated book-burning episodes rather than on lynching. The great Alexandrian library had been burned by Roman soldiers long before Hypatia's day, and during her lifetime the valuable library in the temple of Serapis was sacked by an Alexandrian mob.

Hypatia has been the subject of much romantic drama and fiction, including the 1853 novel *Hypatia, or New Foes With an Old Face,* by Charles Kingsley. Such works have perpetuated the legend that she was not only intellectual but also beautiful, eloquent, and modest.

Bibliography

See T.L. Heath, *History of Greek Mathematics,* II (Oxford, 1921), 528–529: A.W. Richeson, "Hypatia of Alexandria," in *National Mathematics Magazine,* **15,** no. 2 (Nov. 1940), 74–82; Socrates Scholasticus, *Ecclesiastical History,* VII (London, 1853), 15; *Suidae Lexicon,* Ada Adler, ed., I (Leipzig, 1928), 618; B.L. van der Waerden, *Science Awakening* (New York, 1961), 290.

EDNA E. KRAMER

Post-Reading Activities

A. Remembering **facts:**
From your reading—
1. What do you know about Hypatia?
2. What do you know about Orestes?
3. What do you know about Cyril?

B. Learning new **facts:**
Match the names of people with the best description of them.
1. neoplatonic philosophers
2. Euclid
3. Charles Kingsley

_____ 19th-century novelist

_____ philosophers who built a system based on the ideas of Plato hundreds of years after his death

_____ a Greek mathematician famous for his work on geometry

C. For a group **discussion:**
Do you believe the story of Hypatia, Orestes, and Cyril could be the basis for a film or TV miniseries? Why? Why not? Decide on:
1. What famous actors/actresses should take the key roles?
2. Who should be the director/the writer/the producer?
3. Where should the film be photographed?
4. What type of music would be appropriate?
5. What should the costumes look like?
6. What are the major conflicts between the key roles?
   a. Is Hypatia only "beautiful, modest, and eloquent"?
      What are her weaknesses and faults?
   b. Is Cyril only narrow-minded and bigoted?
      What are his good points?
   c. Is Orestes simply the good-looking hero?
      What conflicts does he have about his relationship with Hypatia?

D. Hold a contest. Write a title for a TV mini-series or film about the story of Hypatia, Orestes, and Cyril. Elect three judges from the group to pick the winning name.

Third and Fourth Selections
Guide Books to Alexandria

Pre-Reading Tactics

A. Learning about places in the world and events in history makes us want to travel. Suppose you could go to the city of Alexandria today. What would you find there? What would you read to prepare for the trip?

Travel guides are good reading material both while traveling and when staying at home. Selections Three and Four are up-to-date guides to the modern city of Alexandria. Reading them might make you want to take a trip there . . . or somewhere else.

B. Reading **in-depth:**

Selections Three and Four will give you a chance to experience "reading two books at the same time" since they both cover the same information. Reading one reinforces your reading of the other. Try it. It's an effective technique for learning new information.

C. Remembering **names and places:**

In Selections Three and Four you will find out a bit about the 2,000-year history of Alexandria. You will also encounter some new names and places.

New Names	**New Places**
Cleopatra	the Pharos tower and lighthouse.
Julius Caesar	
Marc Antony	
Octavian	
Archimedes	
Claudius Ptolemy	
Hellenistic (Greek)—remember Helen of Troy?	

Alexandria: Ancient Queen of the Mediterranean

1   Egypt's second largest city and chief port, Alexandria (in Arabic *Is-kandariyah),* is 110 miles northwest of Cairo on the Mediterranean. Its excellent beaches, climate and lively atmosphere have long made it the country's major summer resort.

2   When Alexander the Great conquered Egypt in 332 B.C., he founded a city bearing his name on the site of the tiny fishing village of Rakotis, facing the rocky island of Pharos. Under the Ptolemies, the city grew rapidly and remained the capital of the Empire throughout their reign.

3   The city also became a great cultural center and attracted the most famous scientists, scholars, philosophers, poets and artists of the time. It had two celebrated royal libraries, said to contain 490,000 different scrolls. Around the museum housing one of the libraries rose what is considered one of the first universities in history. Under Ptolemy II, the great Tower of Pharos, one of the seven wonders of the ancient world, was built. The Tower, 220 feet high and lighted by night, is said to have been the world's first lighthouse.

4   During the time of Julius Caesar, Alexandria became the second largest city of the Roman Empire. When Octavian entered the city in 30 B.C., after the suicide of Anthony and Cleopatra, it became formally a part of the Roman domain. Under the Byzantine Empire, Alexandria was one of the great centers of Christendom and see of a patriarchate.

5   By the time the city fell to the Arabs in 642 it had declined considerably. In 1798 when Napoleon's troops landed in Egypt, Alexandria was a mere village.

6   The city regained its importance once more under Muhammad Ali. In 1819 he ordered the construction of the Mahmudiya Canal to the Nile, thus bringing large areas in the city's vicinity under irrigation. Under Muhammad Ali's successors, Alexandria became the traditional summer capital of Egypt.

7   Today, Alexandria has a population of about four million people and is one of the chief seaports on the Mediterranean Sea. Very little remains of the city's ancient past. Remnants of its one-time glory, especially the Greek and Roman periods, are housed in a museum in the center of the city, and excavations continue to turn up important finds, such as the almost perfect Roman amphitheater uncovered only a few years ago.

8 Alexandria is different from Cairo—its ambience is Mediterranean rather than Oriental. If you imagine it as the city described by Lawrence Durrell in his *Alexandria Quartet,* you may be disappointed to learn that it is no longer the same. But Alexandria has a charm and romance of its own, and no trip to Egypt is complete without a visit to this famous city.

Coastal Road and Beaches

9 The first and most remarkable look a visitor can have at Alexandria is the sweeping view of its crescent shaped seafront, lined with stately palms and lovely old houses, hotels and buildings.

10 A 15-mile east-west road, the Corniche, skirts the city along the Mediterranean from the port on the west to Montazah at its farthest limits on the east. From the western end at Ras el Tin, the peninsula that was once the Island of Pharos, the road passes the city's major hotels and cafes on the south to Midan al Tahrir (Liberation Square), the main square of the downtown area overlooking the eastern harbor, and Ramleh, the main tram station. On the far side of the harbor, the road continues along the Mediterranean to the city's most beautiful residential sections on the south and a series of beaches on the north. Many of the beaches have the same names as the city districts behind them: Chatby, Cleopatra, Sidi Gabr, Rushdi, Stanley, Glymenopoulo, San Stefano, Sidi Bishr, Mandara, Montazeh.

11 Here cabins may be rented for the summer season. On both sides of the Corniche Drive, hotels, nightclubs, sidewalk cafes and restaurants are the center of activity for the thousands of Egyptians who spend the summer here.

12 In bygone days, the entire government moved from Cairo to Alexandria for the summer, and the diplomatic corps gladly moved with it. Now the country no longer indulges in this extravagance.

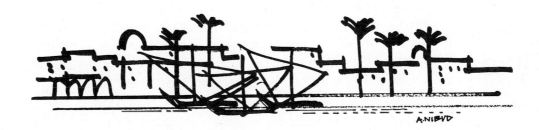

A.NIBVD

Alexandria and Mediterranean Coast: Alexandria

1   To the Western ear the very phonetics of the word are exotic and enticing—*El Iskandaria* in Arabic, the name springs from the tongue like a passing desert breeze. In the mind's eye you might see the gleam of the surreal azure ocean washing the sands before you, as well as images of Alexander the Great, Cleopatra and the Pharos Light-house, one of the seven wonders of the ancient world. But once drawn to Alexandria you will fast awaken from the reverie. As Egypt's second-largest city, with six million inhabitants, modern Alexandria faces many of the same problems as Cairo: overpopulation and a deficient urban infrastructure. Dirt and decay blanket nearly every building, and widespread poverty is painfully omnipresent. Yet these unappealing similarities with Cairo exist in Alexandria to a lesser degree. Ten or fifteen degrees cooler than Cairo in the summer, Alexandria's 18km of public and private beaches make it a popular summer vacation site for residents of the capital and other inland towns.

2   Alexandria was founded in 332 B.C.E. by Alexander the Great, who envisioned it as the capital of his empire, a center of Hellenistic culture, and a major naval base. Though Alexander died before the city was completed (he is buried somewhere near the center of town), Alexandria continued to develop under Ptolemy I, the Macedonian general who inherited the Egyptian empire. The Ptolemaic dynasty ruled Egypt for nearly 300 years with Alexandria as its capital. During this period the city rapidly grew into a major port on the trade routes between Europe and Asia, becoming one of the most important centers for Hellenistic and Semitic learning in the ancient world. Some of the greatest scientists of the day, including Euclid, Archimedes, and Claudius Ptolemy, worked in Alexandria's museum and research institute. The museum's library was said to contain 500,000 volumes, and in it were produced some of the most important scholarly works of the age, including the first critical edition of Homer and the Septuagint (the first translation of the Hebrew Bible into Greek).

3   The last of Alexandria's Ptolemaic rulers was Cleopatra. Seeing Rome's power grow while Egypt's diminished, she turned to foreign affairs with Julius Caesar, who visited Alexandria in 47 B.C.E. When he was assassinated, she allied herself with Marc Antony, the apparent heir to the Roman Empire. Their subsequent marriage scandalized Rome, and especially Caesar's great-nephew Octavian: Antony was already married to Octavian's sister. When, in 30 B.C.E., Octavian defeated Marc Antony in the ensuing power struggle, Cleopatra committed suicide in Alexandria, and the city passed to Roman control. Alexandria remained the capital of Egypt under the Romans and became the most powerful of the Roman provincial capitals. In the second century C.E., the Christian community in Alexandria founded a catechetical school, which became one of the most important theological centers of the early church, under the leadership of Clement of Alexandria and his successor, Origen (who took "if thy right eye offend thee . . ." so seriously, that he castrated himself). In the third century C.E., Alexandria's research institute and library were burnt in a civil war, and the city began to decline as an intellectual center. In 391 C.E. a subsidiary library, in which many schol- ▶

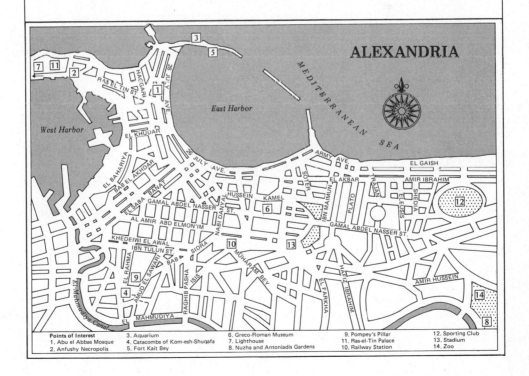

ALEXANDRIA

MEDITERRANEAN SEA

East Harbor

West Harbor

Points of Interest
1. Abu el Abbas Mosque
2. Anfushy Necropolis
3. Aquarium
4. Catacombs of Kom-esh-Shuqafa
5. Fort Kait Bey
6. Greco-Roman Museum
7. Lighthouse
8. Nuzha and Antoniadis Gardens
9. Pompey's Pillar
10. Railway Station
11. Ras-el-Tin Palace
12. Sporting Club
13. Stadium
14. Zoo

ars had taken refuge, was burnt by the Christians. The destruction of Alexandria's libraries was perhaps the greatest intellectual catastrophe of the Greco-Roman period. In 616 C.E., Alexandria was captured by the Persians, and thirty years later by the Arabs. Under Arab rule the capital of Egypt was moved to a site near present-day Cairo, and Alexandria became a minor naval base. Yet another historic misfortune befell the city in 700 C.E., when the colossal Pharos Lighthouse, the ancient wonder which had illumined the port, lost its lantern and ceased to function. Earthquakes in the eleventh and fourteenth centuries destroyed the structure entirely. Finally, when the Portuguese discovered the South Sea route to India in 1498, the spice trade shifted away from Alexandria and with its last remaining *raison d'etre* gone, the city was soon deserted.

4   The city of Alexandria did not really begin to revive until the reign of Muhammad Ali in the early nineteenth century. Between 1818 and 1833, a new canal gave Alexandria access to the Nile, docks and an arsenal were built, and industry began to develop. In the mid-nineteenth century, Alexandria was linked by rail to Suez. With the opening of the Suez Canal in 1869 and the construction of new harbor facilities in the 1880's, Alexandria's position as a principal port was assured. Today Alexandria is a major industrial center and the largest port in Egypt. Because of its beaches and mild climate, it has also become Egypt's summer capital, the city to which wealthier Egyptians flock when Cairo gets too hot.

Post-Reading Activities

A. Remembering **facts:**

1. According to the guide books, the following ruled Alexandria at different periods of history. Put them in the correct chronological order, beginning with the earliest. Use numbers 1–6.

_____ early Christians   _____ Greeks   _____ Persians

_____ Egyptians   _____ Arabs   _____ Romans

2. Based on all of your reading, what other peoples lived in, passed through, or traded in Alexandria over more than 2,000 years?

_____

_____

B. Comparing **information:**

1. You had already read about the destruction of the great library of ancient Alexandria when you saw the same facts mentioned in the guide books. In which paragraphs in Selections Three and Four is the library mentioned?

   Selection Three: _____

   Selection Four: _____

2. Do the three authors all give the same facts? Fill in the matrix (chart) below. In some places you will need to use NI (no information).

	Carl Sagan	**Selection Three (Guide Book)**	**Selection Four (Guide Book)**
Number of scrolls			
Number of libraries			
Other buildings			
Date of destruction			
Cause of destruction			
Other details			

C. Use the map:

   If you visited modern Alexandria, you might want to visit some historical sites.

1. Find the Pharos Lighthouse. Is it actually there today?
2. Where do you believe the famous library of Alexandria was located?
3. Where would you go to see remnants of ancient Alexandria?
4. Suppose you had three days in which to visit modern Alexandria. How would you spend your time? Work out a schedule of your daily itinerary. Compare your itinerary with your partner's. Or, work with a partner and plan how you would spend the time together. Remember, you're tourists on holiday!

Excerpt from *The Alexandria Quartet*

Pre-Reading Tactics

A. The final selection in *Reading on Purpose* is unlike all the others since it is a work of fiction. It is a story created by a writer who wants to entertain and delight the reader. Writers of fiction are artists with words. They weave together facts, information, description, opinions, ideas . . . and tell a story at the same time. When their work continues to be read for many years, then it is often considered "literature."

B. Selection Five is a brief passage from a novel about the city of Alexandria before and during World War II. (A novel is a long, complex story with numerous characters.) The author, Lawrence Durrell, is a famous British writer. In all, he wrote four books about Alexandria called *The Alexandria Quartet*. Find the reference in Selection Three to *The Alexandria Quartet*. Can you guess in what ways the city might have changed?

C. This passage is the first page-and-a-half of the third book in the Quartet, *Mountolive*. Mountolive is the name of the main character in the book. From his name, can you guess what country he is from?

D. Vocabulary Awareness—Durrell uses words to create pictures in the reader's mind. Look for words that describe:

Mountolive's clothing (paragraph 2):
   once-crisp tennis flannels and college blazer
the pace of the story (paragraphs 3, 4)
   turning slowly . . . at the pace of prayer or meditation
the colors (paragraphs 3, 4)
   black reed spines, a screen of gold and violet, lilac afterglow
the sounds (paragraphs 3, 4)
   voices . . . sounded, his own cough, the splatter of geese honking

Mountolive

by Lawrence Durrell

I

1   As a junior of exceptional promise, he had been sent to Egypt for a year in order to improve his Arabic and found himself attached to the High Commission as a sort of scribe to await his first diplomatic posting; but he was already conducting himself as a young secretary of legation, fully aware of the responsibilities of future office. Only somehow today it was rather more difficult than usual to be reserved, so exciting had the fish drive become.

2   He had in fact quite forgotten about his once-crisp tennis flannels and college blazer and the fact that the wash of *bilge* rinsing through the floor boards had toe-capped his white *plimsolls* with a black stain. In Egypt one seemed to forget oneself continually like this. He blessed the chance letter of introduction which had brought him to the Hosnani lands, to the rambling old-fashioned house built upon a network of lakes and embankments near Alexandria. Yes.

3   The *punt* which now carried him, thrust by slow thrust across the turbid water, was turning slowly eastward to take up its position in the great semicircle of boats which was being gradually closed in upon a target area marked out by the black reed spines of fish pans. And as they closed in, stroke by stroke, the Egyptian night fell—the sudden reduction of all objects to *bas-reliefs* upon a screen of gold and violet. The land had become dense as tapestry in the lilac afterglow, quivering here and there with water mirages from the rising damps, expanding and contracting horizons, until one thought of the world as being mirrored in a soap bubble trembling on the edge of disappearance. Voices, too, across the water sounded now loud, now soft and clear. His own cough fled across the lake in sudden wing beats. Dusk, yet it was still hot, his shirt stuck to his back. The spokes of darkness which reached out to them only outlined the shapes of the *reed-fringed* islands, which punctuated the water like great pincushions, like paws, like hassocks.   ▶

Mountolive—cont'd

4   Slowly, at the pace of prayer or meditation, the great arc of boats was forming and closing in, but with the land and the water liquefying at this rate he kept having the illusion that they were traveling across the sky rather than across the alluvial waters of Mareotis. And out of sight he could hear the splatter of *geese,* and in one corner water and sky split apart as a flight rose, trailing its webs across the estuary like seaplanes, honking crassly. Mountolive sighed and stared down into the brown water, chin on his hands. He was unused to feeling so happy. Youth is the age of despairs.

Post-Reading Activities

A. Understand word meanings through **context:**

Paragraph 2

Bilge is	dirty water.	_____
	clean water.	_____
	spilled soup.	_____
Plimsolls are	shoes.	_____
	sandals.	_____
	boots.	_____

Paragraph 3

A punt is	a boat.	_____
	an animal.	_____
	a friend.	_____
Bas relief is	aid to refugees.	_____
	sculpture on buildings which does not stand out.	_____
Reed-fringed refers to	high seas.	_____
	high grass.	_____
	high spirits.	_____

Paragraph 4

Geese are	fish that live in water.	_____
	birds that live without water.	_____
	birds that live near water.	_____

B. Understand the writer's **implied meanings:**

The writer paints a portrait of the main character by giving clues. Find words and phrases which describe Mountolive's:

Age	Social Class	Profession	Current Mood
a junior		*attached to the High Commission as a sort of scribe*	

C. Understand the writer's **spirit:**

Write your responses to these questions. Be ready to talk about your reactions to this kind of fiction writing with others in your group.

Paragraph 3

The world mirrored in a soap bubble on the edge of disappearance.
Based on this passage, do you think the book emphasizes description of place, people, or events?

Paragraph 4

Youth is the age of despairs.
Do you think the story is about a young man or an old man?
Is the writer a young man or an old man?

Part 4 Reading for Personal Discovery

Becoming a successful reader depends a great deal on getting into the habit of reading. This means you must read frequently and for pleasure. You must follow your own reading interests. In *Reading on Purpose* you have read a number of selections which were chosen *for* you. Now it's time for you to find your own materials for reading. By doing so you will take responsibility for your own success as a reader; you will be reading for personal discovery.

Some reading you select for yourself will be for learning, some will be for pleasure or recreation. Since your purpose for reading is not always the same, the way in which you read the material will differ. When you read-to-learn, you should look for main and supporting ideas, trying to remember facts and details. You will probably read the material more than once. On the other hand, when you read for pleasure, you should try to read much faster, not worrying about unknown words. Adjusting your reading style to your purpose is an important part of becoming a skillful reader.

Where will you look for reading materials? In a school library. In a community or neighborhood library. You can share and trade books and magazines with others in your class. Your ESL or English teacher should be able to help you locate materials for reading.

Use the pages in Part IV to keep a record of what you read in English. As the record pages begin to fill up, you will feel your confidence as a reader grow.

I. Sources for Reading-in-Depth

Other materials I have read which deepened my background knowledge about the topics in this book:

Topic	Title of Selection in This Book/Unit No.	Additional Material: Author Title	Type

II. Types of Reading Materials I Selected for Myself

	Topic	Name of Publication Title	Author	Date of Publication
Magazine Articles				
Newspaper Articles				
Books: Non-Fiction				
Books: Fiction				
Textbooks				
Other				

III. Topics for Personal Reading

Topics I have read about in materials I selected myself:
1.

2.

3.

4.

5.

6.

Topics I want to read about in materials I will discover for myself:

Vocabulary List

A

Words and Expressions	Unit	Selection
AMA	Ten	I
accessories	Three	I
a compulsive spender	Three	III
a lemon	Three	II
abuse	Eleven	I
abyss	Nine	II
acceptance	Ten	III
accurate	Twelve	I
ad nauseum	Eight	I
adhere to	Five	I
adversity	Ten	II
albeit	Six	I
alleviated	Nine	III
ambivalent feelings	Six	I
anger	Ten	III
anguish	Nine	II
anxiety	Ten	III
anxiety tremors	Seven	IV
appalls	Ten	I
apprehend	Nine	II
articulate	One	II

B

bad-mouth	Two	I
baffled	Six	II
bittersweet revenge	Ten	II
bizarre	Eight	I
blunted	Five	I

Words and Expressions	Unit	Selection
blurred by my angry tears	One	II
bondage	Three	IV
brittle	Five	I
burned	Two	III
buying into	Ten	I
by virtue of exclusion	Ten	I

C

cardiovascular disease	Eight	II
(a) catch to it	Four	II
centennial year	Five	II
centrifugal force	Six	III
chagrined	Six	II
charge	Four	I
chasm	Six	II
checkout	Three	II
chipped	Five	I
chronic insomnia	Ten	II
chronicle	Six	III
civility	One	I
collision	Three	II
communal	Eleven	I
communicate	Six	I
competition	Six	I
composure	Ten	II
contorted	Six	II
converting	Five	I
coping (dealing with)	Ten	III
creativity	Nine	I
culprit	Seven	IV
culture of Narcissism	Eight	I

D

daily routine	Eight	II
a deal	Three, Four	I, II

Words and Expressions	Unit	Selection
dean of boys	One	I
dehumanized	Ten	III
demise	Five	II
depreciation	Three	I
detoxification center	Seven	IV
diminutive	Five	II
disgruntled	Nine	I
dismay	Nine	I
dismiss	Nine	I
dominating	Five	II
drum up	Four	II
dubbed	Five	II

E

educational system	Nine	I
egotistical	Ten	I
endeavour	Two	III
(enduring) frustration	Six	I
envy	Six	I
ethnic group	One	I
execrable	Eight	I

F

factors	Eleven	I
famine	Nine	II
fanfare	Seven	IV
fatality	Ten	III
finesse	Two	I
flirted	Ten	II
flunk	Two	I
flux	Nine	II
fly in the face of	One	III
form of deviance	Eleven	II
fossil	Five	II
frugal	Four, Six	IV, II

Words and Expressions	Unit	Selection
G		
get hooked	Eight	I
get off their duffs	Eight	II
glib line of gab	Two	I
(to) go for	Four	II
grasp	Nine	I
grievances	Eight	I
groping	Six	II
guilt-ridden	One	II
H		
hailed	Eight	II
handful	One	I
hard-core	Eight	II
health benefits and health risks	Eight	II
heed	Two	III
holds sway	Nine	II
hormones	Six	III
hypnotized	Eight	IV
I		
ideosyncratic interpretation	Five	II
illiterate	One	II
impact	Five	I
imperil	Eight	I
in the market for	Four	I
indentured	Eleven	I
indispensable	Seven	IV
innovations	Nine	I
interpretation	Thirteen	I
intervene	Eleven	I
intimidating	One	I
irreconcilable	Five	III
isolation	Eleven	II

Words and Expressions	Unit	Selection

J

jealousy	Six	I

L

leap	Seven	I
leap year	Five, Twelve	II, II
let it slide	Seven	I
liability	Eleven	I
liberation	Three	IV
likely	Thirteen	I
lunar	Twelve	I
lunar month	Five	II

M

market executive	Four	I
(in the) market for	Three	I
market value	Four	III
marketing	Four	I
martyr	Ten	II
me decade	Eight	I
meager	Ten	III
Medicis	Four	III
meet high standards	Nine	I
mind goes blank	Two	I
morbid	Ten	III
mundane	Six	II
my stomach churning	One	II

N

nascent	Six	I

Words and Expressions	Unit	Selection
O		
obliged	Seven	I
off guard	Two	I
omnipotence	Ten	III
on the defensive	Two	I
ooze	Thirteen	I
open-sesame	Four	III
oppression	Nine	III
options	Three	I
overbearing	Eight	II
overdue	Seven	IV
P		
paean	Seven	IV
paleontology	Five	II
papal bull	Five	III
paradox	Three	IV
pebbles	Ten	III
perceptual/astronomical	Twelve	I
perplexed	Five	II
physical exertion	Eight	IV
piece of prose	Six	II
plagued (with)	Ten	I
play the game	Two	I
precipitating	Eleven	I
prejudice	One	I
prep course	Six	III
presides	One	I
pride	Six	I
proficient reader	One	II
prompts	Seven	IV
protest (v.)	Eight	I

Words and Expressions	Unit	Selection
R		
racial bigots	One	I
racism	One	I
(for) real	Four	II
rebel (v.) rebellion (n.)	Ten	II
rebellious	Seven	I
receded	Thirteen	I
reconciling	Five	III
red-blooded	Seven	IV
rehashes	One	III
relieves	Nine	II
restrictions	One	III
reverberated	Nine	II
revoked	Eight	IV
rim	Nine	II
ripples	Thirteen	I
rivalry	Six	I
rot	Seven	IV
rust	Three	II
S		
scavenge	Eight	II
scorched	Two	III
secondhand	Three	II
sedated	Ten	III
sedentary	Eight	II
segregation	One	I
self-expression	Nine	I
sever the . . . cord	Seven	IV
sex ratio	Eleven	II
shallow	Thirteen	I
shape up	Eight	IV
shatter	Five	I
shocks	Three	II
Shylock	Four	III
shop around	Eight	IV

Words and Expressions	Unit	Selection
sibling	Six, Ten	I, III
singed	Two	III
small talk	Two	I
smoking gun	Thirteen	I
smug	Ten	I
solar	Twelve	I
solar year	Five	II
speculation	Thirteen	I
statistics	Eleven	II
status quo	Three	IV
stems from	One	II
stomped	One	II
strains	Seven	IV
succumb (to)	Five	II
surge of resentment	One	II
surmise	Ten	I
suspension hearing	One	II
syndicate	Four	III

T

taboo	Ten	III
take for granted	Nine	I
tangible	Eight	II
tatterdemalion	Three	IV
taunted	Eleven	I
telephone addiction	Seven	IV
telephone-aversive heart	Seven	IV
test-drive	Three	II
the fate of (dinosaurs)	Five	II
to be programmed for	Seven	IV
to cope (with)	Ten	II
to dicker over	Three	II
(to) lament	Eight	I
to opt	Three	II
to prove your mettle	Eight	I

Words and Expressions	Unit	Selection
to qualify	Eight	IV
tombstones	Ten	III
train (of thought) de-railed	Seven	IV
trendies	Eight	I
truculence	Three	IV

U

ubiquitous	Three, Seven	IV, IV
unearthed	Five	II
unfathomable	Nine	II
unprofitable	Seven	I
unveiled	Eight	II
up for grabs	Six	III
uproot	Six	II

V

validity	Thirteen	I
valuable precedent	Five	III
vanished	Five	II
verge	Nine	II
vernal equinox	Five	II
vitality	One	I

W

wayward	Nine	II
weekly pay check	One	II
well-being	Eight	IV
words fail her	Six	I

Acknowledgements

Text Credits

Unit One

pp. 4-6, Copyright © 1984 "Learning to Live Peacefully in a High School Melting Pot in New York" by Sara Rimer of May 17, 1984 by the New York Times Company. Reprinted by permission.

pp. 13-15, Enriquez Hank Lopez

p. 17, Copyright © 1984 "Immigrants Place No Strain on the American Environment" by George P. Mann, of May 18, 1984 by the New York Times Company. Reprinted by permission.

Unit Two

pp. 21-22, Scripps Howard News Service

pp. 26-27, Diane Angel Emberlin, *Los Angeles Times*

p. 30, Copyright © 1940 James Thurber © 1968 Helen W. Thurber. From *Fables of Our Times,* published by Harper and Row.

pp. 32-35, © 1985 by Frank Donegan and reprinted with permission of Penthouse International Ltd.

Unit Three

pp. 38-40, "How to Buy a New Car" from Sylvia Porter's *New Money Book for the 80's.* Copyright © 1975, 1979 Sylvia Porter. Reprinted by permission of Doubleday & Company, Inc.

pp. 42-43, Reprinted by permission from the March 1981 issue of *McCall's.*

pp. 47-49, Copyright © 1974 by *Harper's Magazine.* All rights reserved. Reprinted from the 1974 issue by special permission.

p. 51, Courtesy First Wisconsin Corporation

Unit Four

p. 57, Reprinted with special permission of King Features Syndicate, Inc.

pp. 60-62, From *The Money Lenders* by Anthony Sampson. Copyright © 1981 by Anthony Sampson. Reprinted by permission of Viking Penguin, Inc.

pp. 65-66, Courtesy *Glamour,* Copyright © 1984 by The Conde Nast Publications Inc.

Unit Five

pp. 70-71, Reprinted by permission of *American Way,* inflight magazine of American Airlines, copyright 1985 by American Airlines.

pp. 74-75, Bettyann Kevles

pp. 79-80, Isabel R. Plesset who is the author of the book *Noguchi and His Patrons*.

Unit Six

pp. 85-86, Paul O'Brien

pp. 89-91, Mabel Wong Hogle

pp. 95-96 Ellen Goodman 1985 Washington Post Writers Group, reprinted with permission.

Unit Seven

p. 100, Debra Hotaling, reprinted from *Los Angeles Times*.

p. 103, Taken from ''Dear Abby'' by Abigail Van Buren, copyright © 1982, Universal Press Syndicate. Reprinted with permission. All rights reserved.

p. 105, Leticia (Tish) Baldridge

pp. 108-109, Thomas H. Middleton

pp. 111-112, Ellen Goodman, 1985 Washington Post Writers Group, reprinted with permission.

Unit Eight

pp. 116-118, Copyright © 1980 ''The Boston Marathon: Passing of an American Pastime,'' by Art Carey, by the New Times Company. Reprinted by permission.

pp. 122-124, Reprinted from the October Issue of *Science* 84 © 1984 by the American Association for the Advancement of Science.

pp. 126-127, Courtesy of the New York Hilton

pp. 128-129, Peter D. Lawrence, first published by *Esquire Magazine*

Unit Nine

pp. 133-134, Kei Ho

p. 136, George Allen and Unwin Publishers Ltd.

pp. 140-142, From *Cosmos* by Carl Sagan. Copyright © 1980 by Carl Sagan. Reprinted by permission of Random House, Inc. and Copyright © 1980 by Carl Sagan Productions, Inc. Published by Random House, Inc. Reprinted by permission of the author and the author's agents, Scott Meredith Literary Agency, Inc. 845 Third Avenue, NY, NY 10022.

Unit Ten

p. 148, Judy Lane McDaniel

pp. 151-152, Joan Friedberg

pp. 156-160, Reprinted with permission of Macmillan Publishing Company from *On Death and Dying* by Elisabeth Kübler-Ross, Copyright © 1969 by Elisabeth Kübler-Ross.

Unit Eleven

p. 163, *Readers Guide to Periodical Literature* copyright © 1985 by the H.W. Wilson Company. Material reproduced by permission of the publisher.

pp. 164-165, Reprinted with permission from *Psychology Today Magazine*. Copyright © 1985 American Psychological Association.

pp. 168-170, From *Introduction to Sociology,* by Daniel Hebding and Leonard Glick. Copyright © 1976 by Newbery Award Records, Inc. Reprinted by permission of Random House, Inc.

Unit Twelve

pp. 174-179, From *The World Book Encyclopedia*, © 1986 World Book, Inc.

pp. 182-183, © 1980 by Houghton Mifflin Company. Reprinted by permission from *The American Heritage Dictionary of the English Language, New College Edition*.

Unit Thirteen

p. 185, *Readers Guide to Periodical Literature* copyright © 1985 by the H.W. Wilson Company. Material reproduced by permission of the publisher.

pp. 186-190, First appeared in *Science Digest* © 1983 by The Hearst Corporation.

Unit Fourteen

p. 193, Reprinted with permission of *The Encyclopedia Americana* © 1986 by Golier, Inc.

Charles C. Gillispie, editor, excerpted from *Dictionary of Scientific Biography*, Volume VI. Copyright © 1972 American Council of Learned Societies. Reprinted with permission of Charles Scribner's Sons.

pp. 196-197, Reprinted with permission from the book *Fodor's Egypt* copyright 1986. Published by Fodor's Travel Guides.

pp. 198-200, *Let's Go Israel & Egypt* by Harvard Student Agencies Inc. Edited by Claire Landers, copyright © 1986 by Harvard Student Agencies Inc., St. Martin's Press, Inc., New York.

pp. 203-204, From *Mountolive* by Lawrence Durrell. Copyright © 1958 by Lawrence Durrell. Reprinted by permission of the publisher, E.P. Dutton, a division of New American Library.

Every effort has been made to locate the authors of these selections but regrettably this has not been possible in every case.

Art Credits

pp. 9-10, Christopher Blumrich and Art Staff *Newsweek*

pp. 12, 17, 52, 122, 190, 193, 197, Catharine O'Neill

p. 76 "The Far Side" cartoon is reprinted by permission of Chronicle Features, San Francisco

pp. 96, 104, 113, 159, 185, Ahsile Nibud

p. 99, Walter Fournier

p. 126, "Route for Runners" by Sue Siegel

p. 199, Map by Robert C. Forget

Photo Credits

pp. 6, 83, Christopher Columbus High School

pp. 20, 146, Ralph P. Turcotte

p. 41, Courtesy of Volksvagen

pp. 48, 117, *Salem Evening News*

p. 69, British Tourist Authority

p. 94, Kathy and John Boehmer

p. 175, The Pierpont Morgan Library, M.399, f.10V-11

p. 176, Mrs. G. Andreas Garson